Brew
IT
Yourself

PROFESSIONAL CRAFT BLUEPRINTS
FOR HOME BREWING

How to READ this book

CHOOSE YOUR VESSEL

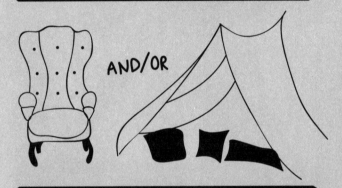

AND/OR

CHOOSE YOUR ALLY

Brew It Yourself

Brew It Yourself

Professional Craft Blueprints for Home Brewing

Erik Spellmeyer & Jamie Floyd
First Printing, October 1, 2014
All text is © Erik Spellmeyer & Jamie Floyd, 2014
This edition is © Microcosm Publishing, 2014
All photos by Meggyn Pomerleau, except where noted,
taken at F.H. Steinbart Co. in Portland, Oregon.

In the DIY series

Microcosm Publishing
2752 N Williams Ave
Portland, OR 97227

For a catalog, write or visit
MicrocosmPublishing.com

ISBN 978-1-62106-665-1
This is Microcosm #161

Distributed worldwide by PGW and in England by
Turnaround

Edited by Joe Biel and Lauren Hage
Designed and illustrated by Meggyn Pomerleau
Fonts by Ian Lynam
Cover by Meggyn Pomerleau

This book was printed on post-consumer paper by
union workers in the United States.

FOR MY FATHER,
Craig Robert Spellmeyer

TABLE OF CONTENTS

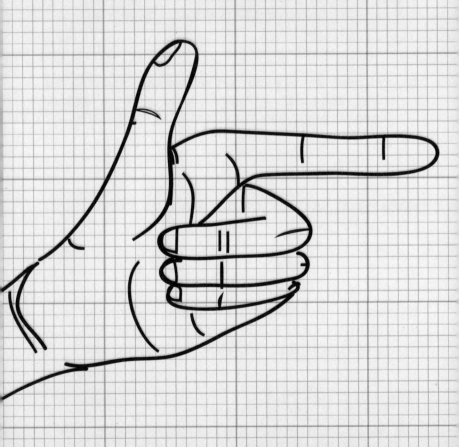

Foreword

by Jamie Floyd

What is your connection to beer? If you've made it this far you are connected to beer in some way. Human relation to beer is as old as our ability to write words. It has followed us through millennia on our journey towards modern civilization and helps us understand our past.

My first memories of beer are of my dad's moisture-covered Coors can on the back porch table on a hot Summer day in Cupertino, California. He didn't drink often, but when he did, he drank Coors Original. Because of this, Coors reminds me of the carefree days of being a kid and spending time with my family. But to my dad, who spent five of his seven years in the Air Force stationed in Alaska, beer was a way to pass the frigid days away. I found a picture of him with his military buddies proudly huddled next to a five-foot pyramid of empty Coors cans, carefully stacked.

Because of this, my family avoided the snow. My love of beer and snowy conditions wouldn't start until I fell in love with snowboarding and a perfect pint of cask-conditioned Jubelale from the Deschutes Brewery Pub during my college days in Oregon. Catching twelve inches of fresh snow with some big carving fat airs, great friends, a meal, and a pint of tasty ale at the end of the day warmed me up in the pub. I still think of these fond memories every time I take a sip of Jubelale. On the rare occasion I taste a Coors, I think of my dad. Why is beer such an emotional reminder of other times in our lives?

Beer is the third most consumed beverage in the world behind water and tea and the most consumed alcohol in the world.

That's right—more beer is consumed than coffee. Beer is as old as our conception of society and has helped us become the people we are today. Beer is one of the first things in history that humans made for themselves, unleashing nutrients from grains, making water potable, and easing the tensions of the day. Our fascination with beer has endured for millennia and, after the relatively quick disruption of prohibition, is enjoying its real Renaissance as a partner in human existence as we now have the informational tools to share with each other all the secrets of this delicious concoction. We can taste beer from all over the world, use ingredients grown in other countries, and read passionate stories about our love affair with beer. The Craft Beer Movement in the U.S. and abroad has unleashed the power of beer and its many facets, flavors, histories, novelties, and passions. There are now over 3,500 breweries in the U.S. with another 1,900 being planned. Not since long before Prohibition we have had so much contact with different kinds of beer. Curiosity is turning into hobby and for people like myself, hobbies are turning into careers.

I would have never guessed 25 years ago when I first brewed a batch of beer that I would later own a brewery, explore other brewing regions of the world, judge beer professionally, teach others about beer, or write a foreword for a brewing book. My desire to serve my community, teach others, and produce something that is shared by those around me is fulfilled with beer. Where will curiosity take you, my friend?

I made my first batches of beer in the kitchen of the Lorax Student Housing Cooperative located near the University of Oregon campus with my friend Russell. We made five gallon extract brewed beers that were downright mediocre but were loved by our friends. We had less knowledge about making beer than is in this book. Brewing beer is not very complicated to make, but making it taste good can take some time.

It is sometimes hard to remember the days before access to the awe-inspiring amount of information we have now, but in 1994, a computer could help you find a book in a library but not the definition of an ale or lager. As for brewing books, you might be able to find *The Joy of Home Brewing* written in 1984 by Charlie Papazian, but that was about it.

Russell and I purchased the necessary equipment at the local home brew shop, which Erik writes about in the chapter on extract brewing. One great thing about brewing your own beer is that as you get more sophisticated with your brewing technique, most of what you buy can still be used with the new equipment. The owner of the brewing supply store was somewhat helpful by making kits and pointing us in the rightdirection, but beers back then were limited to English Bitter or Stout. We had limited access to yeast strains as well and many were dry, which was further limiting.

It was a few years before I knew that breweries like Ninkasi give yeast strains to home brewers in the community. There were no "clone recipes" yet to try to recreate your favorite beers and there were few craft breweries for role models. Red Hook, Widmer, Full Sail, Sierra

Nevada, and Portland Brewing made most of the bottles you could find and Deschutes was only a draft beer back then. McMenamin's High Street Brewery was around when I arrived in Eugene but Steelhead, where I would later work, was not open until 1991. We would try them all and any imports we could find. Imports were easier to find than local breweries, leading to my love of European styles as much as my NW IPAs.

Brewing was a fun hobby for friends to figure stuff out on our own and share the results. Snowboarding, hiking, gardening, cooking, going to concerts, being a Sociology geek, and playing Dungeons and Dragons were hobbies that I gave equal attention to, in addition to a full course load of college classes and a couple of jobs. Despite that schedule, I found the time to brew some beer.

Before the Craft Beer Movement, our understanding of beer was that it was made by big U.S. companies and I thought most of the Imports must be made by big companies as well. Protestant-inspired reform and prohibition isolated U.S. citizens away from our past and connection to beer. In 1887, the U.S. had 4,131 breweries—its all time high. As competition and a consumer tendency shifted towards lighter European Lager styles, U.S. breweries dropped to around 1,000 breweries before the Prohibition era started in 1920. When Prohibition ended in 1933, there were upwards of 750 breweries that shrank to 400 in the early 50s and declined further to around 80 in the 80s, as breweries were competitively put out of business or absorbed into larger companies. By this point, every brewery was producing a similar light lager beer that is still the predominant beer in the U.S.

The 20th century was a period of forgetting deep-rooted, cultural connection to a variety of beers. It wasn't until Jimmy Carter legalized home brewing in 1978, and courageous new brewers opened breweries, that we started to reconnect to our past connection with beer. Humans learn quickly and—now with the technology to share and transmit endless amounts of beer-related information—we have a deeper understanding of our relationship with beer, providing us with a promising future. You can develop and perfect the recipes in this book until your heart is content.

Humans have likely been making beer since about 9500 BC, when Neolithic folks were starting to grow cereal grains. Archeologists found chemical evidence of a grain-based beer dating back to around 3500 BC in the Zargos Mountains of Western Iran. Early Sumerians were common in this area as it was on the Silk Road Trade Route. Cereal grains would be planted, and the nomadic tribes would keep moving to hunt and gather and look for water, returning to harvest the crops. As time went by, these early brewers saw that brewing beer made water potable because any beverage with more than 2% alcohol will not allow pathogens to grow. Brewing retrieved more nutrients from the grains harvested, as the fermentation process converts starches into usable sugars while also allowing us to access the vitamins in the beer grains, making beer a staple food for humanity.

So there you have it: BEER IS FOOD!

As time passed, and beer became more important to the nomadic tribes, they realized that carrying around beer ingredients was labor intensive, so some tribes started to settle in areas and grow grains to make bread and beer. The Sumerians were one of the first of these nomadic-turned-agricultural tribes and they settled about 80 miles south of Bagdad in what is now Iraq. They made beer and worshiped the Goddess Ninkasi for the miracle of fermentation. These brewers acted as a cultural hub to early civilization. As different groups of people started settling in the same area, the need for a better way to communicate became necessary and the early Sumerians created written language through Cuneiform characters on clay tablets. With this added tool of communication they created schools, laws, and taxes. Beer became an early form of trade. In the Sumerian outpost of Elba around 2500 BC, there is evidence that the area made beer of many different recipes and consumed quite a bit every day. Some of this evidence indicates that one of the beers may have been named Elba after the city where it was made. It may have been the first brand of beer! The Tablet of Alulu found in the city of Ur from around 2050 BC contains the oldest known receipt for beer delivery. The first written food recipe is the Hymn of Ninkasi, which is a prayer to the Goddess that also contains instructions to make beer. The early Sumerians were quick to start writing oral traditions to spread knowledge faster and more accurately. As they developed the ability to articulate through writing, they developed stories about beer.

If you have only enjoyed beer as a consumer, take the next step—follow this book and make a beer. When you brew beer, you begin to understand what makes a beer good and what changes the flavors. Brewing your own beer gives you empathy for the brewers who make the beers you love. Every experience I have with brewing gives me a better appreciation for how others have honed their craft. Once you truly understand the art and science of brewing, you can share that knowledge with others while also sharing the passion for good beer.

Learning to brew is learning one of humanity's oldest skill sets; one that was almost lost. In our modern world we no longer have to be taught how to hunt, farm, make soap, or even cook, if you have the resources to avoid it. These former survival skills have become hobbies. Sociologist Emile Durkheim wrote of Homo Habilis as a sociological idea that talks about how we find meaning in ourselves by the things we create. We find deep satisfaction when we create something with our own hands. Whether you brew in your kitchen, garage, or backyard, all these spots are welcome places for company to come and share the knowledge, fun, and work it takes to make beer. Sometimes we drink as much beer as we make in a day but it is fun and our friends love being a part of it. My college friends can say they drank my first beers with pride when they order a pint of my beer at the bar. So what are you waiting for? There is fun to be had, knowledge to be learned, friendships deepened, histories told, and futures written!

So mash in and brew on, fellow citizen!

Intro

duction

I remember my early introductions to beer as unexpected and slightly embarrassing. It wasn't uncommon to find my dad, conquering the weekend in the company of a cold bottle of suds. Weekends were good times; cold, refreshing beverages were too. At the time, my palate was only familiar with enjoying the pleasures of cold juice, lemonade, the occasional pop, and of course, cold milk; it was not prepared for the utterly unfamiliar and unauthorized sip of a bottle, alone on a table, while my dad's back was turned.

I saw my father's beverage as a satisfying solution to my hot summer's thirst, and while his eyes were elsewhere, I helped myself to a nice big slug. Not expecting this new, not-fruity flavor, I spat out the dry, bitter, and altogether awful froth, drawing my dad's attention. In my surprise and revulsion, I dropped the bottle on the floor, where it glugged out a shameful pool. My father, confused, flustered, and mourning the loss of his beer, threw his hands in the air and continued to chuckle at my expense. Needless to say, it was some time later that the stigma of beer transformed into something to enjoy with relaxing ease.

I grew up in St. Louis, Missouri, home to the "King of Beers": *Budweiser*. The facility is massive; its name is everywhere. One of the main icons of my youth is the flaring neon Anheuser-Busch eagle illuminating the side of Highway 40, observed on every return from Busch Stadium, home of the St. Louis Cardinals and once on August 21, 1966, The Beatles. It was relatively difficult to escape the influence of Budweiser beer: little league sponsorship, immense promotional campaigns, and random rubbish on the side of the road. You really felt singled out with such slogans as, "this Bud's for you." Perhaps this is where my relationship with beer began; from spilling my dad's Michelob Dry, living in the constant shadow of the brewery, the ever-present "bought and paid for" beer belly as common as the city's summer humidity; this was my culture. It's no big surprise then, that by the time I was old enough, I made my way out of my general aversion for beer and onto a path that became an obsession for the next decade of my life.

From the time the law would allow, I'd be on the search for what my palate would deem the perfect beer; seeking out restaurants and bars that advertised an unusual selection of draft and bottled beer. However, the home of the "King of Beers" had a social monopoly on the selection and the diversity was a little lacking. Being aware of the surging microbreweries all along the coasts, I followed the manifest out to Eugene, Oregon where I began home brewing on a "more than recreational" level, seeking out others who did the same and enhancing my overall knowledge of beer. I sampled literally hundreds of different beers, designed and made by commercial breweries, microbreweries, home brewers, and friends.

I became obsessed with beer culture, both historical and contemporary. My favorite place to go in Eugene quickly became the famed Bier Stein. This place, to my underdeveloped and over-inflated fervor, did more than provide ample selection; it culminated a collection of knowledge, passion, and libation, the likes of which I hadn't expected. There were more bottles than I could count; each of the many coolers, which lined the walls, represented a different country, sometimes a different region. This place offered an aggregate to a higher learning.

It was easy to occupy an evening with a solid dedication to a different country's beer. The western United States alone was a daunting task. My passion was to understand the modern India Pale Ale (IPA). West of the Rockies, humble brewers have been hard at work establishing the protocol for what many consider to be the flagship and testimony of the microbrewery. This trend has caught on in a major way; the popularity of this style is validated in nearly every microbrewery in the USA. What was once merely a clever method to preserve the fresh flavor of the English Pale Ale on its long journey to India has become one of the most popular styles of beer in the world. With its in-your-face bitterness and fruity aroma, its simple design has inspired a revolution, a liquid uprising that replaces wine at many meals.

During one of my evenings at Bier Stein, we were breaking into the many indulgences of the Belgians. This was my first "Trappist" beer. Someone at our table confirmed that my preconceptions of monks brewing all the beer for all of Europe, while ludicrous, had some foundation in fact. Belgium is not only home to some weird-looking sports car manufacturers, they also set the ridged guidelines for what is known as "Trappist Breweries." For a beer to bare the Trappist insignia, it must be made by monks. There's a fair amount of other guidelines: the brewing must be secondary to their faith, they can't really be in it for the profit, and it has to be brewed within the walls of the Trappist monastery. According to the powers that be, there are currently only ten of these breweries in the world, most of them in Belgium.

As my knowledge grew, my desire to drink every beer in the world slowly shrank, beset by my accumulating awareness of how insane the menu would be. I had a new dream: I wanted to work at a brewery. This would be much better for my finances. I worked my way up the social ladder and landed myself a job at a then up-and-coming microbrewery in town, *Ninkasi.*

I began learning all that I could about large scale micro brewing; everything from washing kegs, hauling out spent mash, and the glory of pouring buckets of hops into a boil. I was in a dreamland of aroma, hard work, and beer. I also had the privilege of meeting some of the great names in the business; I hobnobbed with beer enthusiasts from every corner of the beer-loving world. I learned how truly massive the industry was. It is in honor of these experiences that I write this book to encourage the ongoing reputation of beer.

Preface

Even if you don't have much interest in drinking beer, basic knowledge about the age-old tradition of making your own beer can increase your understanding of the people around you. There's a historical tradition whose particularities may intrigue you even if you never intend to boil your own wort.

There is a tremendous amount of conflicting information out there about the "right" way to make the quintessential beer. So rather than add noise to that argument or attempt to be the definitive authority on all beer, this book is about finding ways to get involved, and places to start making beer at the level that is comfortable and appropriate for you, while discovering where your interests lie.

Some say that *Technology Brewing and Malting* by Wolfgang Kunze is the best, but it's written in a way that assumes you have a degree in micro or macro biology, and is fairly spendy. And as anyone who has attended a party can attest to, everyone has different tastes. So that's why this book can give you a realistic understanding of the process of brewing beer, meeting you where you're at, and producing a beverage you can enjoy and be proud of.

Think of this book as a resource that connects you to other resources. But let's assume that you want to brew beer in order to drink it. This book will provide you with enough information to let you create your own conclusions and familiarize yourself with your tastes, to see which methods are ideal for you. Outlined here are the most common methods used in brewing, along with their shortcomings and advantages. You'll learn about jargon used in the industry and basic terminology that is used casually in and around the brewing of beer.

Some recipes out there are quick and easy and some are a little more involved. Even if you don't have a prior understanding or much experience, by the time you finish reading you should have enough understanding to improvise upon or alter recipes you find elsewhere.

This book works best if you read it in order.

Skills build upon each other and the resources in this book make the most sense in the order that they are presented, even if you already think you have a specific interest further in.

Bolded words in the text appear with accompanying definitions along with their first appearance but if you run into a word that you can't remember the meaning of, you can also reference the glossary in the back.

Erik Spellmeyer

Useful diagrams and charts in this book:

Now let's get some ideas brewing!

In consideration of the most common....

ONE MALT EXTRACT HOME BREWING

This is among the most common for the non-commercial, non-professional home brewer. It involves, more or less, the same four ingredients as its more complicated associates: malt, water, yeast, and hops. The essential difference is that the primary malt source is an extracted syrup, liquid, and/or a dry powder. Malted barley or other grains can be added for enhancing the flavor profile or beefing up the body, however most recipes ordered or purchased through home brew shops or online will consist of a malt extract.

TWO ALL-GRAIN HOME BREWING

This is the preferred method of a more involved home brewer. There is more room for creativity and potential freshness since there is no malted extract to profile the beer. Your grain profile hinges on the combination of malts you choose.

THREE COMMERCIAL MICRO-BREWING

The advent of commercial micro-brewing created a surging industry of small batch beers occupying a water source near you. The brewing method differs predominantly in the volume and capacity of the tools used in the process of all-grain home-brewing.

FOUR COMMERCIAL BREWING

Typically in American Lager format:

Budweiser, Coors, Pabst, Miller...

Again the major difference is, you guessed it, **size.** The brewing methods are utilizable in the smaller home-brewing capacity.

CHOOSING YOUR HOME BREW METHOD:

The two most commonly utilized methods of home brewing are typically referred to as all-grain and extract brewing. The two are comprised of nearly the same ingredients and equipment, and yield what some would say are similar results. As you read on, we'll look at the subtle and not-so-subtle differences to understand what's best for you.

EXTRACT
BREWING

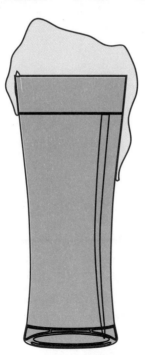

Ok, did you go out and buy the tools and read all the right book on home brewing? Before you do or in case you haven't, this chapter will introduce you to all the things I wish I knew before I put together my first home brew.

First, we'll deal with *extract beer.* What exactly is being extracted? *Malt.*

The beauty of making extract beer is that you don't have to:

* *MALT YOUR OWN GRAIN*
* *MILL YOUR OWN GRAIN*
* *MASH YOUR OWN GRAIN*

A *concentrated malt extract* is a sweet-tasting concentration of sugars from mashing, the process of heating a mix of *milled grain* and water. What results is the wort, the liquid extracted from the mashing process. Either by applying heat or by using a vacuum, the concentration is made; the result is either a thick, liquidy syrup or a dry powder, depending on how much water is removed. Most home brewers prefer to use the liquid extract, as it is said to provide a fresher-tasting beer, however the freshness of the beer depends on the freshness of the extract. The liquid extract has a shorter shelf life, so it is often fresher. If you intend to brew right away, liquid makes sense. If not, a dry malt with a longer shelf life may make more sense.

If you're making an extract beer, it's likely to be packaged with a recipe already put together by your local home brew shop or by the manufacturer. More sources for recipes can be found online.

A typical package has a container of your malted extract. The amount will vary from brew to brew, but you can expect about eight pounds, more or less, for dry or liquid extract. Depending on the recipe, you might have some specialty-malted grains to add for your *mash*, or steeping process. Varying ounces of *hops*, a flavoring and stability agent for the beer, will be included. Hops come in different forms as well. The most common in home brewing is called a *hop pellet*. They look like a large bright-green fish-food pellet or rabbit food pellet. There's also fresh or whole hops. The difference is a matter of preference; they each have advantages and regardless of which you end up using, you will have a delicious beer, made by you!

Perhaps the most important and interesting ingredient is the yeast. Brewers yeast can come in many different packages and forms. My favorite idea is called a "smack-pack," made by Wyeast Laboratories. It's a pouch within a pouch, housing live yeast cells. The outer pouch is home to another liquidy bath, so when you smack the pouch—hard enough to burst the inner pouch—the two substances combine to add to your beer batch for instantaneous fermentation! Pretty cool! Yeast can come in many different forms. The home brew shop near you likely has the basics, but there are many ways to utilize the properties of yeast. Play around and experiment; it's only beer! There are the optional water agents that may be included, but for the most part, the organic materials are essentially four things:

water, malt, yeast, and hops!

DRIED WHOLE HOPS

DRIED HOP PELLETS

Every brewer will tell you something different about water. I have dabbled in different water agents, and with a chemistry degree, I'd have probably made the most out of these differences. Most brewers will say that the quality of your water is the essential backbone to a healthy and delicious beer. Some turn their nose up at tap water; there are some places that have terrific tap water, like Portland, Oregon where I live. Every water source will vary, i.e. some will have additives like flouride, so it's always a good idea to know what you're drinking. These additives can have desirable or undesirable effects on the home brewing process. Taste your water, turn it into a party, a-b it to a bottle of filtered spring water, and note any similarities of differences. Does it have a metal flavor, or does it taste like a public swimming pool? Use the *Brew Log templates* to mark down your observations. Check out some of the brew forums on **homebrewtalk.com** and ask around. Look into your local water source and ask questions. If there's one thing this book hopes the reader will find edifying, its that you are totally in control!

Here are a few water agents brewers find useful:

- **IRISH MOSS:** This can be used to enhance the clarity of your finished beer.

- **CALCIUM CHLORIDE/EPSOM SALT/ LACTIC ACID:** These are commonly used to alter the water profile, such as the hardness of your water, or the pesticides or minerals it does or doesn't contain.

Pragmatism ———————————————

The tools can be simple or complicated and as hi-tech or low-tech as you want. Beer has been around and in many forms for thousands of years. The Mesopotamians probably weren't using very complicated equipment and they still drank beer. Use what ya got, get creative in your simplicity, or go big—it's your world! Maybe you want all of the cool stuff right away. But more likely, the more you get into it, the more you will recognize how fancy gear can simplify your problems and what tools you should buy.

Ok, you've got your recipe in a bag on your counter. What now? Assuming you're making the typical five-gallon batch, the first thing you're going to need is a nice pot or kettle that holds at least seven gallons. As they say, steel is real. You can use an aluminum pot, but the steel is worth the extra money. This pot, or brew kettle is necessary for your strike water. Your *strike water* is the initial water used to create your mash or *steep*, a similar process to mashing, used to extract colors and flavors from certain grains. This water must arrive at a relatively precise temperature in order to properly steep your grains. The ideal strike target temperature is typically recommended in the area of **152–160°F.** This is where a fancy floating thermometer comes in handy. These trusty plastic thermometers are made tough and sturdy. They conveniently float in your liquid and arrive at a temperature you can depend on. You can also purchase a digital probe thermometer for even more precise measurements. It features a long wire probe, which is quite optimal. You're gonna need a big, long spoon, and a carboy too. A *carboy*, or *fermenter*, is a large glass/plastic container for storing and fermenting beer. If you don't have a carboy or any interest in buying one, any multi-gallon container will work. Plastic buckets or coolers are ok, but the genius of the carboy is the lovely tapered top, ideal for attaching an air lock. Any container you use would ideally be able to let air out without letting it in. Once you add or pitch the yeast, the brew will go crazy! It produces a lot of carbon dioxide gas. You want to keep unwanted impurities in the air out of your beer, but also allow those gases to escape. As long as this can happen, you'll get what you want. As you can imagine, *air locks* come in many forms and can be as simple as a sealed hose attached to the fermenter, leading into a bucket of water *(see drawing-right)*, or as fancy as a two chambered, S-shaped device that plugs into the top of your vessel. When it's time to make the purchase, your local homebrew shop will provide you with all the options.

So you've got the vessels to cook and store your brew. What else? Some other handy necessities may include a funnel, strainer, and *siphon*. Depending on how scientific you want to make your brew, a *graduated cylinder* and a *hydrometer* will aid in keeping track and knowing the alcohol content of your brew. Some people use a stove, others use a turkey burner ($40-$115), or a propane burner. Whatever you use, know that you're going to have to bring around five gallons of liquid up to a rolling boil. Keep that in mind when choosing where to set up your brewery.

Fast Forward!

Your beer is brewed, you've moved that cooked beer into your fermenter, your yeast is pitched, and your air lock is attached. Fast-forward a few weeks. What now? It's time to move that beer again to either your secondary container for further conditioning and clearing the beer, or you can leave the beer where it is for the full fermentation and siphon or rack the beer directly into your preferred vessel: bottle, keg, or open vat for party time! Ready to go? Let's go through an extract brew together, step-by-step, using the most ideal equipment in my brewery, aka my kitchen.

Let's get brewing!

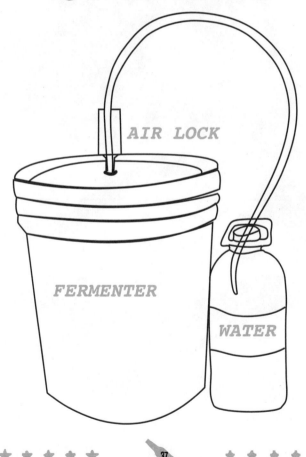

2 Chapter

GETTING DIRTY WHILE BEING EXTREMELY CLEAN

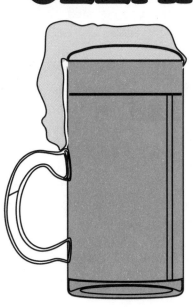

Bacteria and impurities can be the death of a good-tasting beer. Everything that comes in contact with your brew must be sanitized. There are many ways to accomplish this. *First, get your brewing area free of unnecessary clutter.* An organized start will lend to a clean finish. *Once your brewery is free of unwanted mess and is looking nice and organized, it's time to start sanitizing.* I like to keep an open sink, or a large-volume container of sanitized water. Some people use a spray bottle of iodine solution, others like to submerge each item in a prepared vat of sanitizer solution; the "dip solution." Whichever you choose, remember that you're cleaning anything that comes in contact with the beer, not the beer! That's why I prefer the simple single step sanitizer, an oxygen-based cleanser (found at any home brew shop), and the dip method. The advantages are in the name; no rinse is necessary. The spray bottle method works well to keep your hose contacts and multi-use tools clean. The real beer doctors use rubber gloves, or my favorite, nitrile gloves. You can imagine how one can get swept away with cleanliness. *Find your happy place and try not to drop your spoon on the floor before stirring the mash with it, or at least sterilize it first!*

Here We Go!

Extra malts/grains are sometimes used to beef up the body profile of the beer, in addition to the malted extract. The most efficient method for most kitchens is to start with a two to two and a half gallon container of strike water, the initial water used to steep the mash. You can also do what's called a *full boil*, bringing nearly six and a half gallons of water to a boil. This can take a long time if you don't have a strong burner, and can waste energy. You would also have to adjust other factors, like your hopping schedule, when you are going to add your hops. Mess around, if you like a hoppier beer, this could be the right way for you. Keeping it simple, we'll start out using the two and a half gallon method.

Remember your optimal strike water target temperature is *152–160°F*; any higher can bring unwanted reactions with the grains and one reaction can cause the destruction of vital starches and sugars necessary for fermentation.

Bring the water to a slightly higher temperature initially, before adding grains, to give yourself time to get things ready while the water cools to the ideal temperature in your recipe. Use your thermometer. Adding the grains will lower the temperature, so factor that in as well.

OK! You've got your water ready. I've found that putting the grains in a *grain sock* or cloth bag—found at your home brew shop—keeps things nice and tidy. If it fits your personality better, you can always pour loose grains in, but extract brewing has the advantage of having already gone through the mashing process, so some recipes that add specialty malts are only for beefing up the flavor profile.

It's Wort Time!

Wort (PRONOUNCED WERT) is the stage of the liquid that is not quite beer. This weird German word refers to the result of steeping grains in your strike water for anywhere from **30-90 minutes.** The resulting fluid is your wort. Steeping the grains pulls out body and flavor for your beer. It also adds a base of sugars from the starches in the grain, which will convert into alcohol during fermentation. Remember, you want to keep that strike water as close to the target temperature as possible. If you have a precise stove, you can keep a heat source on it, being careful not to overheat. I like to put a lid on it, keep an eye on the temperature, and relax. For me, relaxing is getting everything prepped and clean. Thirty minutes of down time is an excellent opportunity to get all your brew tools sanitized.

It's Extract Time!

Timers are terrific friends for a brewer. There's nothing quite like a boiling, foaming, scorching batch of what was to be a delicious beer, gone to waste because you were busy reading The New Yorker… Sometimes it's too easy to sit and come up with caption ideas for the cartoons… Ok, thirty minutes have passed and it's time to crank up the heat. Now that you've produced your wort, it's time to produce your beer. At the moment you have between two and two and a half gallons of wort.

We're making a five gallon batch, so, here's what we're going to do:

- Add water until the liquid level is up to approximately **five and a half gallons.** We need to get the loose grain or grain bags out of the wort. This can be a little tricky, but with the help of some convenient tools, it'll be just fine. I like to use a sanitized one-gallon milk jug to approximate my water additions. You are going to perform a *sparge*, a weird Latin word that means to scatter the residual sugars out of the grain. We'll use one of my favorite tools, a fine porous strainer with a sturdy handle (you don't want it to buckle and splash hot wort in your face.) to scoop out the grain sacks (sanitize first!).

  Pop Quiz: What's the temperature of that skin burning splash?

- Lifting the bags out of and above the wort and using the milk jug, pour the water over the grain sacks to rinse, or sparge. Continue to sparge until you have approximated **five and a half gallons** and bring the pot to a boil. Lifting the bags out of and above the wort and using the milk jug, pour the water over the grain sacks to rinse, or sparge. Continue to sparge until you have approximated **five and a half gallons** and bring the pot to a boil.

You now have a lot of heavy grain in a sack. It becomes spent grain at the point when it has been rinsed/sparged to its desired end and deprived of most of its sugar potential—the Germans would disagree, as they will use the same grains for more than one brew. If you own a cow, or know someone who does, what's left of the grain might make a great snack for them. If not, maybe you have a compost pile.

★ ★ ★ ★ ★   ★ ★ ★ ★ ★

Once you have reached a nice-looking boil, it's time to add eight pounds of malted extract. This addition will go a lot smoother if you remove the pot from the heat for a moment while you pour and stir in the malt. Try to pour and stir at the same time, and do it slowly. You can use a little warm water to swoosh around in the malt container to get all that sweet syrup into your brew.

That was a clean spoon, *right?*

⊢——Now We're Brewin'!

Answer from previous page:
152-160F

Once you've got that malt nice and mixed in, bring the pot to a rolling boil. Set your timer to **60 minutes** from the boil. Relax, stir occasionally to avoid scorching, and get those hop additions ready.

Hops: Nice little alpha acid containing bittering/ preserving agents. Suspected of having their existence first mentioned (ostensibly) by *Pliny the Elder*, and their first cultivation sown by, you guessed it, the Germans.

If you're using whole hops, grains sacks are convenient and will keep things from getting messy. Alternatively, hops pellets more or less just absorb into the boil and don't leave a mess.

Some recipes have one hop addition, others may have three, four. Let's assume that your recipe has two. Typically, a recipe will follow a strict hopping schedule so use your timer. Now that our 60-minute timer has been set—at the time of the boil—it's time to add the first aromatic hop pile, commonly referred to as the bittering hop addition. We're getting there! At the addition of these hops, I like to set an additional timer which indicates when there are about **10–15 minutes** left of my boil. This is when you add the last of the hops. This addition is commonly called the finishing hop addition.

★ ★ ★ ★ ★ ★ ★ ★ ★ ★

We're close!

Once the 60 minutes are up, it's time to cut the heat. Remove the kettle from the heat because it's time to cool the beer down. Take a sanitized strainer and remove any hop sacks. It's time to introduce one of my favorite brewing tools, the `wort chiller`. This beauty is a coil of copper tube with an in line and an out line. Both ends have a hose attachment; the line in attaches to your water source and the line out will drain down your sink or into your garden, if you like. Once the outside is sanitized, place it inside your kettle and turn on the water. The cool water passes through the chiller, lowering the temperature of your wort rapidly, cutting down your wait time significantly. These copper companions can be spendy, but they are worth it if you're making beer frequently. Shop around and you can find one for around $100. The alternative—filling your sink or bathtub with an ice bath for your kettle—can take a long time. Some brewers prefer it, as it can make good use of your sanitizer water, and sometimes the old ways can be the best ways. And if you choose this method, take a clean spoon and stir the beer, allowing rapid contact with the walls of the ice-cold kettle.

While waiting for the wort to cool, sanitize your carboy or fermenting vessel. Use your thermometer to bring that lovely liquid to the ideal pitching temperature (`pitching:` adding your yeast). When you transfer the wort into your fermenter it will bring that temp down, so again, factor that in when pitching your yeast. If you are feeling strong, you can pick up the whole container with your wort and pour it through a sanitized funnel into the fermenter. If that sounds strenuous or too potentially messy, use a siphon instead. Either way, keep track of your temperature.

wort chiller

hydrometer

funnel

cloth bag

cornelius kegs

tools of the

stainless steel kettle

mash tun

thermometer

bottle cappers

carboy cleaning brush

spoon

TRADE

strainer

s-shaped airlock

carboy

Once your wort is in the fermenter, it's time to pitch that yeast! Add the yeast into the container with the wort. Then, sitting on a comfy chair, place the fermenting vessel on your lap, and shake it vigorously back and forth for a minute or so to agitate your concoction. This gets the yeast saturated in the wort, and is the best and only time you want to *oxygenate/aerate* (forcing fresh oxygen into the liquid) your brew. This is an important step, as oxygen is essential for the yeast in the fermentation process, as most of the oxygen was removed during the boil. There are a few different methods that utilize some more fancy gear, but I prefer the old way, and the least expensive. Now that you're worn out, it's now time to attach the air lock and store your fermenter.

Next, you are going to ferment your beer somewhere around room temperature. Fermentation, at its best, occurs around **68°F**. Recipes for different beers and yeast will differ a little, but you should not let your fermenting beer get above **90°F**.

If you're using a clear vessel, direct light can damage your beer.

Find space in a closet or an out-of-the-way but indoor location, as this process can take a month or longer. Wrap your fermenter in a blanket to keep out the light and keep the beer warm. Depending on the style of beer you've brewed, your ferment temp may vary a little, but a solid temperature to shoot for is approximately **65°F.**

In the initial stages of fermentation, your beer will off-gas something fierce, releasing CO2 and building a thick, foamy crust known as the *krausen* ("crazy burping foam"). This will last for days, depending on the beer. During this period, the beer passes through the complicated stages from aerobic to anaerobic activity, complicated words to say that the yeast uses oxygen to convert sugars into alcohol, turning your wort into beer! Your recipe will indicate how long the fermentation process lasts. While your beer is setting for one to three months, check on it periodically to make sure bubbles are coming through your air lock. This will be slow at first, then intensify, and you'll know it's finishing when this process slows again. Once your beer has finished fermenting—that is, when the gurgling and churning is done—you can leave it right where it is or move it into a secondary. Some people transfer into a secondary (another carboy) to avoid the dreaded *autolysis*, or yeast cannibalism. This is what happens when the yeast runs out of delicious food to eat, turns on itself, and does the unforgivable, resulting in an off flavor. The yeast will eventually settle into what brewers call a *yeast cake* (not exactly edible). Once fermentation is complete, some people transfer the beer into yet another vessel for clarification, getting rid of the *"chill haze"* or chunks that cloud your beer when it's cooled to the temperature it's ideally served at. If you are transferring it, you have cheap and expensive options. You may pour the beer through a strainer or use an expensive and complicated pump-action filter. The more you brew and experiment with different methods, the more you will know what's best for you.

Guess the country of origin for that word.

★ ★ ★ ★ ★ ★ ★ ★ ★ ★

And now it's time to rack your beer, again moving it from one vessel to another. Some people rack into bottles for final conditioning, which can take from a couple weeks to another month or longer.

Answer from previous page: Germany

What About Carbonation?

If you're using a kegging system, you will use the CO2 from your kegerator. If you are going to bottle, add a little *priming sugar* directly into the beer prior to bottling or a little into each bottle. Different brewers claim different results, but do what feels good and experiment! I found inconsistencies in the carbonation level from adding it bottle to bottle, so I put it into the beer prior to bottling.

Put **two and a half to five ounces** of priming sugar into each **five-gallon** batch of beer. Boil the priming sugar in a small amount of water and pour it into the beer for best results. If you're using a *racking bucket*, a five-plus gallon bucket with an opening/closing valve at the bottom for attaching a hose and siphon, add the priming sugar into the bucket before siphoning the beer.

Now The Fun Part

Using your siphon, fill your bottles and cap 'em! Let them sit in a nice, dark place for another two weeks (or according to your recipe) and get involved.

Capping

It's imperative that you cap your bottles, and cap'em good! Your local homebrew show will sell a capper and caps. The caps are cheap and can be bought in bulk! **Cappers** come in different shapes and sizes and range anywhere from $15-40. There is the stand: Like it sounds, you place the bottle in the stand, attach a cap to the magnetic mechanism and crank down on the arm. The device drives the cap onto the bottle and is quite efficient.

There is the twin lever: This has two arms with a round cup/magnet in the middle where you place the cap. You place the simple machine on top of the bottle and, using both hands, push/pull down on the arms until it is capped.

If this is one of your first batches of homebrew, it might be best to sample the results alone first before subjecting your work to the criticism of others. You never know!

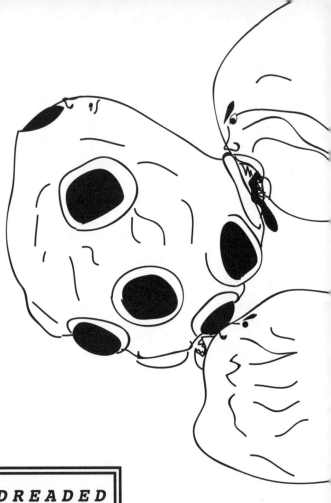

THE DREADED YEAST AUTOLYSIS

Recipes
by Jamie Floyd

Extract brewing is about learning the basics of beer. These recipes are designed to be straight forward with a variety of ale styles to choose from. Each has a different set of things to learn from and develop on.

BASIC GUIDELINES:

- STEEP THE CRUSHED GRAINS IN 1.5 GALLONS OF 160 F WATER FOR 30 MINUTES.
- REMOVE AND SPARGE (POUR LIQUID) INTO THE BOIL KETTLE WITH THE HEAT
- ADD ALL EXTRACTS AND SUGARS TO THE KETTLE AND STIR TO DISSOLVE COMPLETELY.
- CAREFULLY BRING TO A BOIL, STIRRING TO AVOID SCORCHING AND WATCHING FOR BOIL-OVERS.
- ONCE YOU ACHIEVE A ROLLING BOIL, ADD HOPS ACCORDING TO YOUR SCHEDULE AND ANY OTHER ADDITIVES BASED ON THE BREW CLOCK.
- WHEN THE BOIL IS COMPLETE, REMOVE FROM HEAT TO BEGIN TO COOL.
- UTILIZING AN ICE BATH OR WORT CHILLER, BRING THE TEMPERATURE DOWN AS QUICKLY AS POSSIBLE.
- WHEN WORT IS COOLED ADD IT TO A CLEANED AND SANITIZED CARBOY OR FERMENTER.
- ADD WATER UNTIL THE TOTAL VOLUME IS 5 GALLONS IF NECESSARY. THIS WATER SHOULD HAVE BEEN BOILED AND COOLED AHEAD OF TIME SO THAT IT IS STERILE.
- ONCE WORT GETS BELOW 80 DEGREES, TAKE A HYDROMETER READING AND THEN AERATE (SHAKE UP) THE FERMENTER WELL AND PITCH (ADD) IN THE YEAST. WHEN PRIMARY FERMENTATION IS DONE AND THE KRAUSEN OR FOAMY HEAD RECEDES, AND BEER BEGINS TO BRIGHTEN UP, RACK TO A SECONDARY FERMENTER.
- PRIME AND BOTTLE, AND IT WILL BE READY TO SHARE.
- IBUS SOUND FANCY BUT ARE JUST UNITS OF BITTERNESS

Blonde Ale
Light refreshing beer

This is one of the lightest ales you can make. It is pleasing to most people and doesn't alienate the new craft beer drinking friend. There is also little for the beer to hide behind so if your brewing process isn't clean, the beer won't be either. This is a great beer to start with. Without big hop or roast flavors, you will learn to master clean fermentation.

1.054 OG

38 IBUS

Extract:

6 lbs. Pilsner Liquid Malt Extract

Grains:

1 lbs. Carmel Vienna

.5 lbs. Munich Malt

.5 lbs. Golden Naked Oats

Hopping Schedule:

60 Minutes: Santiam 1 oz.

15 Minutes: Mt Hood 1 oz.

0 Minutes: Mt Hood 1 oz.

Yeast:

Wyeast 1007 German Ale

1332 Northwest Ale Yeast

Raspberry Golden Ale:

A light and fruity treat.

Some brewers would simply take their blond ale recipe and add raspberries and call it good. This recipe is simple so the raspberry taste comes through. It also has one hop variety which is a good trick when you want to learn about other aspects of the beer, like its malt profile or how fruit might affect the flavor of a beer. By using one hop, if it doesn't taste just right with the berries, than you know which hop to change since there is only one. If you use three hop varieties you may not know what to change.

1.056 OG
30 IBUS

Extract:

5.5 lbs. Pilsner Liquid Malt Extract

Grains:

1.5 lbs. Munich Malt

Fruit:

Raspberry Puree

Hopping Schedule:

60 Minutes: Tettnang 1 oz.

15 Minutes: Tettnang 1 OZ.

0 minutes: Tettnang 1 oz.

Yeast:

Wyeast 1056 American Ale

Wyeast 1968 London Ale Yeast

West Coast IPA:

This is a straightforward IPA with West Coast hop profile.

Everybody loves IPA, right? This is a nice IPA recipe to share with friends who love hops. Centennial and Cascade have been used in many modern IPAs, so when you make this beer it will seem familiar to your friends. In this recipe there are two hop varieties to give it floral and citrusy notes. You can use the same base recipe and different hops to make new IPAs. Adjust the amounts of hops added, based on the alpha acids in the variety and what part of the brew you want to use it in.

Extract:

7 lbs. Pilsner Liquid Malt Extract

Grains:

Crystal 15: 1 lbs.

Honey Malt: .25 lbs.

Biscuit Malt: .25 lbs.

Hopping Schedule:

60 minutes: Centennial 2 oz.

15 minutes: Cascade 1 oz.

0 minutes: Cascade 1 oz.

Yeast:

1056 American Ale Yeast

Wyeast 1968 London Ale Strain

1.050 OG
80 IBUS

Irish Style Stout:

If someone doesn't like IPAs, then they likely will enjoy a good stout. Some people love a good stout year round, not just when it's cold out. This is to make an Irish Stout which is one of the most recognized stout styles. It is the dark malts that give the roasted, coffee, and chocolate flavors we expect in stouts. Notice this recipe has only one bittering hop addition to balance the malt. This style of stout is not hoppy in flavor or aroma. The hop bitterness helps support the bitterness you get from the black patent and roasted malts used.

1.060 OG
60 IBUS

Extract:

6.5 lbs. Light Liquid Malt Extract

1 lbs. Dark Dry Malt

Grains:

.5 lbs. Crystal 120L

.5 lbs. Black Patent Malt

.5 lbs. Roasted Barley

Hopping Schedule:

60 Minutes: 2 oz. Northern Brewer

No 15 or 0 minute addition

Yeast:

Wyeast 1084 Irish Ale Yeast

1469 West Yorkshire Yeast

British ESB:

The extra special bitter is a benchmark of traditional British brewing and is an easy drinking but flavorful beer.

The extra special bitter is the hallmark style for balance and drinkability in England. Bready and toasty malt flavors are matched with earthy and resinous hops flavors to make a remarkably easy to drink but flavorful beer. Using English hops, yeast, and, at times, grains can make a beer taste like an Import. Show your friends how worldly you are.

Extract:

6 lbs. Pilsner Liquid Malt

Grains:

5 lbs. Munich Malt

.25 lbs. 60L

.10 lbs. 120L

.10 lbs. Special Roast

Hopping Schedule:

60 Minute: 1 oz. Fuggles

15 Minute: 1 oz. East Kent Goldings

0 Minute: 1 oz. East Kent Goldings

1.056 OG
40 IBUS

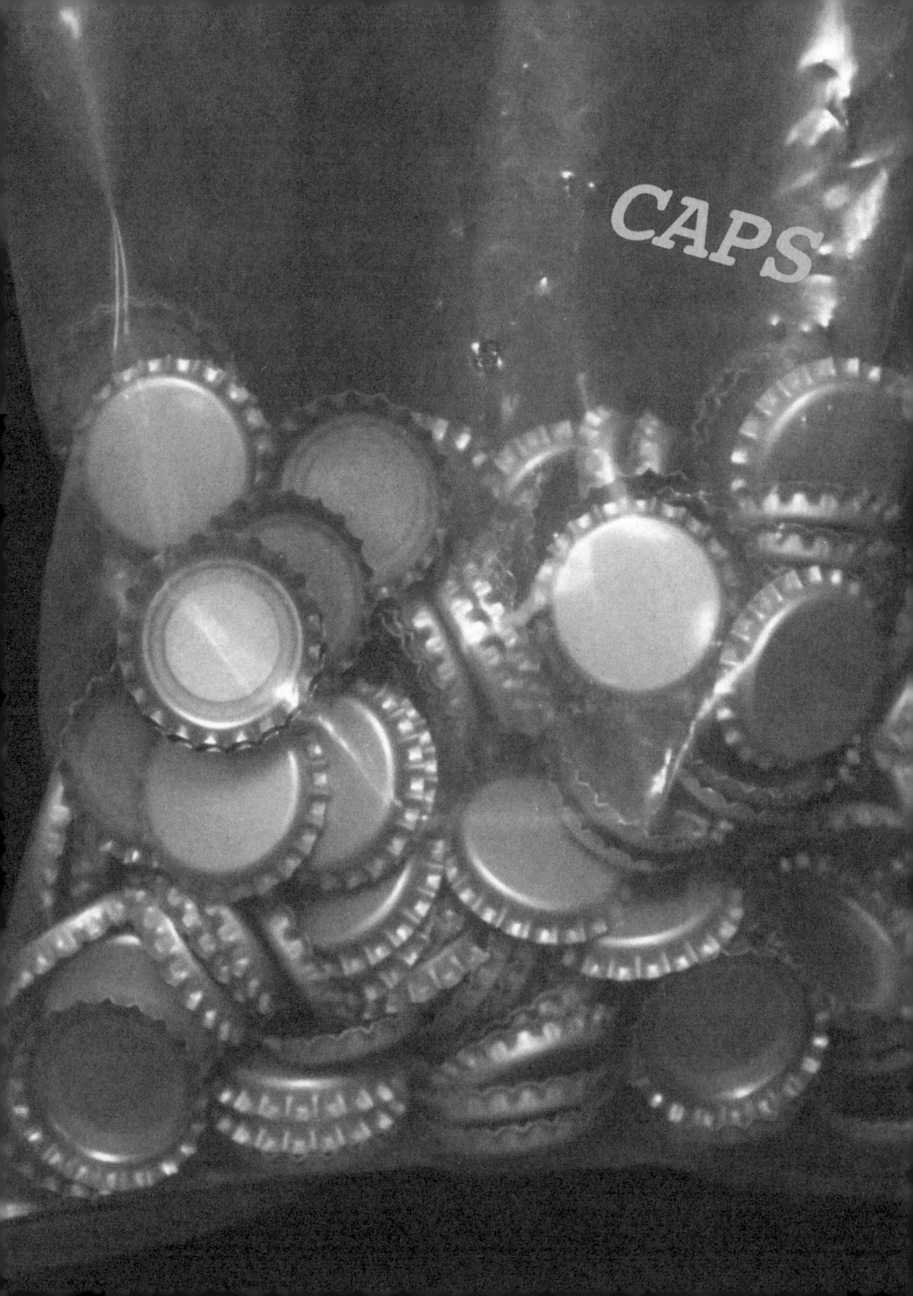
CAPS

chapter

ALL GRAIN BREWING

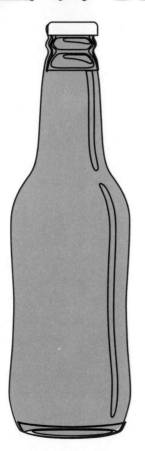

All-grain brewing is a fun and moderately lounge-able way to spend part of the day. Let's talk about, and hopefully demystify, some of the abstract terminology used in the brewing industry. For the DIY universe, we'll talk about what gear is essential, what can be improvised, and what you can make yourself! Depending on your knowledge, what you want out of it, and how you go about it, brewing can be a very expensive hobby or relatively economical. There is some helpful and fascinating equipment out there, but it is rarely necessary and often expensive.

Let's Get Started By Getting Comfortable —|

Whether you're a dyed-in-the-wool DIYer or a slightly assisted hobbyist, all-grain brewing is certainly something to tip your hat to. It can be much more involved than extract brewing and if you'd like, it can be raised to echelons stretching into territory far too complicated to discuss in this book. It can also be as simple as you can make it.

I like to think about beer as a simple thing, a practical elixir once used to sustain the hungry bellies of humble folk. Consider that beer—although perhaps varying from one civilization to the next—is nothing more than fermented organic materials, discovered almost certainly by accident, and no matter what form has been found, it follows a general pattern of simplicity.

As we've discussed, all-grain and extract beer have a similar result. Beer is the desired common denominator and once you've tried your hand at the extract method, you may find yourself feeling more ambitious or simply wanting to make all-grain beer. It's certainly more time consuming than extract beer, and requires a step or so more, and a bit more gear.

Mash Tun and Mashing

The largest piece of gear you'll need to get all-grain'n is a mash tun. We've gone over its cousin process, steeping, but *mashing* is when you add your milled grain and malted barley into your strike water or "liquor."

Hot Liquor Back

A mega-awesome piece of brewer's equipment is known throughout the industry as a liquor back. The beer industry is chalk-full of lingo and fancy terms designed to make your beer taste better! "*Hot Liquor*," known to the rest of us as "hot water," is what is used for the strike. A *liquor back* is a temperature-controlled reservoir, which holds enough "hot liquor," to serve as your strike. It is kept near the mash tun and kettle and home brewers often build tier systems for their brewery, so that gravity feeds the liquid through the brewing cycle.

This device creates an efficient and simple process of mashing-in and starting your boil, not to mention the transition between your mash and your sparge. In the professional brewery, wine, and spirit worlds, the product is often referred to by measurement, using the word "barrel" where **one beer barrel equates to thirty-one U.S. gallons**. "How many barrels of beer are we brewing today?" In the professional brewery environment, the liquor back can be as big as 30 barrels with a working capacity of **930 gallons**.

Mashing-In:

Before the dry grain takes a hot, strike-water bath, the malted barley is dumped into the vessel containing the strike water, ideally a temperature-controlled mash tun. This is *mashing in*. The combination of strike water and malt becomes the mash! This is the wonderful stage where the lovely *diastatic enzymes* in the malt convert the starch in the grains into sugars! These are the same sugars used later by the yeast in the fermentation process to make the favorable alcohol element in the beer. The resulting liquid is now wort!

Remember that you will lose a few degrees once you add the grain/malt, so make the water a few degrees hotter, but also make sure that you are not losing heat in the mash tun!

Method One:

Heat water/strike water to the ideal **152-160°F**. The liquid is going to be in there for a while, so keep a lid on it!

There is a considerable amount of delightfully in-depth opinions on how to control the strike water temperature. For many of us who brew without the luxury of a modern microbrewery, our temperatures will be among the most difficult thing to keep consistent. Whether you're mashing in a state-of-the-art stainless steel mash tun, or a ten gallon Igloo cooler from the hardware store, you'll have to be considerate to your temperature at all times. Consider keeping a **BREW LOG** *(templates can be found at the back of this book).*

Some brewers like to prep-heat their mash tun with hot water. Most DIY mash tuns will lose heat throughout the mash; so this step can help maintain some heat consistency. Think of a coffee mug in the cupboard. It's colder than the hot coffee you're going to add to it, and that coffee will lose some of its heat when it raises the temperature of the cold mug. Those of us who want our coffee as hot as possible add hot water to warm the cup before pouring the coffee! The same principle applies to the mash tun. Add some hot water to the vessel, put the lid on it for a few minutes, and then dump it out before you begin your mash.

The Tun

The mash tun comes in many forms. It can be an all-inclusive vessel that performs the mash, the mash out, raising the temperature of the mash to **170°F**, the lauter, separating into the clear liquid wort and the residual grain, and the sparge. The tun can be as simplistic as a home cooler with an augmented hose and valve.

DIY Mash Tun

Feeling crafty? If you're like most of us, "feeling crafty" is an easy way of saying, "I'm broke and will have to build it myself!" People become surprisingly innovative when it comes to beer. Of the many projects that can improve beer production, building a mash tun is one of the coolest and least expensive. You may even have much of what you need laying around. Remember the part of Thoreau's Walden, when he listed materials and the cost of each, in the construction of his home on the pond? He built himself a home for $28.12! Building a mash tun can be just as economical.

There is plenty of information on-line about creating your own mash tun. Most parts and instructions are universal, as are these instructions. Take a look online to get a good idea of different methods before you get started.

- ### INSULATED TEN GALLON COOLER
  Make sure it has a plug in it, or a liquid release spigot, or you'll have to drill one. I prefer the long, rectangular ones, but many prefer the tall, round ones.

- ### LACED STAINLESS STEEL HOSE 1/2" X APPROXIMATELY 1 TO 1 1/2 FEET
  (similar to water supply lines in a home bathroom)
  You will have to hold this tightly with a vice grip, a vice, or a burly human hand, and remove both ends. A hacksaw is ideal. Once you remove the ends, pull the steel back and pull out the inner plastic lining.

- ### 1/4" STAINLESS STEEL HOSE CLAMPS
  You can use the screw-down clamps or, if you have the fancy vice clamper, use the corresponding clamps. Make sure they're stainless steel!

- ### 1/2" BRASS PLUG OR CAP
  Will be used with the 1/4" stainless steel clamp to plug one end of the braided stainless steel hose.

- ### 3/8" TO 3/8" FEMALE (BRASS) BARB ADAPTOR
  Make sure it's long enough to fit through the hole in the cooler where the plug was, enough to expose the threads. Remove all of the cooler's stock valve components and replace them with the new ones. Keep that in mind when selecting a cooler.

- ### *3/8" MALE (BRASS) BARB ADAPTER WITH A 1" NIPPLE*

  This will attach to the other end of the hose, via the female barb adaptor, using the other hose clamp.

- ### *3/8" FEMALE (BRASS) BARB ADAPTOR WITH 1" NIPPLE*

  This will attach to the end of the next piece.

- ### *3/8" THREADED (BRASS) BALL VALVE*

  This will attach to the outside end of the 3/8" to 3/8" female barb adaptor.

- ### *(3) 5/8" FENDER WASHERS*

  (don't use the ones from your car)

  These will be used as fitting spacers on the inside/outside of the cooler.

- ### *5/8" RUBBER O RING*

  This will be used on the outside of the cooler to form the fitting between the barb adaptor and the cooler.

- ### *SEAL FROM THE COOLER'S ORIGINAL SPIGOT*

  Keep it, as the original seal is the ideal fit.
  This will be used to seal your fittings.

Assembly:

There are great videos on the web that show how to do your assembly. Sometimes it helps to see someone else do something first. If you find these instructions confusing at first, watch a few videos before attempting your own assembly.

Disassemble the spigot on the cooler. Remember that you'll need this part later. Keep all of the parts that you remove, just to be sure.

Prep your double-sided 3/8" brass barb adaptor, wrapping it with a couple layers of Teflon tape.
Replace the original spigot seal.

Insert the double-sided 3/8" brass barb adaptor on the inside of the cooler.

Slide on one of the 5/8" fender washers.

Attach the 3/8" male brass barb adaptor with nipple.
On the outside of the cooler, attach the rubber o ring on the outside end of the double-sided 3/8" brass barb adaptor and set it into place against the cooler, forming a gasket.

Slide on the remaining two 5/8" fender washers.
Make sure there's Teflon tape wrapped around the double-sided 3/8" brass barb adaptor, and attach the ball valve.

Assure that you have a nice, tight seal between all of the fittings and that it's not wiggling against the cooler. If so, you need either more washers or gaskets.

Apply Teflon to your female 3/8" brass barb adaptor with nipple and attach it to the ball valve.

Using a vice or an iron grip, attach both ends of your 1/2" by approximately 1-1 1/2' braided stainless steel hose with a hacksaw.

Pull back one of the ends of the hose to reveal the inner plastic lining. Using your fingertips, or needle nose pliers, remove the plastic liner.

Take one end of the hose and insert your 1/2" brass plug and clamp it to the hose with a 1/4" clamp.
Take the other end of the hose and attach it, using your other clamp, to the inside nipple.

Tools You'll Need:

- **A pair of channel locks or an adjustable wrench.**
- **A hacksaw and a pair of scissors.**
- **Needle nose pliers**
- **A screwdriver or a vice clamp, depending on what kind of 1/4" clamps you're using.**

This completes the DIY mash tun!

A fabulous detail about this mash tun is that it costs around $50 U.S. If you look at what a mash tun costs online or in home brew shops, you might be even more excited about your creation. But what is the stainless steel hose for? It may look odd, but its function is vital. It is the central nervous system of the tun, making it much easier, and even possible, to complete future steps in the brewing process: the three stages of lauter.

But first, it's time to malt!

Malting/Milling

Unless you've malted your grains in a kiln and broken them down into your desired *grist size*, you're going to need to understanding milling before you proceed.

In order for the grain to reach the milling stage it must be malted: *germinated* (the sprouting stage of a seed or spore) by a water bath, and removed and dried at the desired stage. Malting creates enzymes that are later converted into sugars in the mash and a vibrant collection of multi-syllable scientific words that string together to characterize an otherwise straightforward procedure.

It is rare for a home brewer to malt their own grains, it is even rarer still for microbrewers and commercial brewers to malt their own grain (Coors Brewing Co. still malts theirs). A home brewer typically purchases pre-malted grains from an online source or a local homebrew shop. But once you have malted grains, you must mill those tiny kernels before you dump them as is into your hot liquor mash.

Milling is a simple procedure but requires a fair amount of accuracy. The idea is to shape the malt so that the ideal amount of enzymes can be released in the mash. The mechanics of milling go back to the mortar and pestle crushing method, tracing back through the ages of antiquity. The objective is simple: crush the malted kernel to the right shape, to remove some of the husk. The remaining husk forms a filter during the lautering process. Fancy mills can be purchased and manipulated using tools found at home.

Mills found at micro and commercial breweries can be massive, noisy, delicate, and scary. I once hucked huge, heavy sacks of delicious sweet malt into a gigantic, formidable mill. It wasn't possible to dump the entire bag in at once; that would cause the mill to jam or stick. The load must be added at a pace consistent with the mill's capacity.

The crushing burs pulverize the malt, creating grain dust, which fills the air ominously and is hazardous. You're covered in sweat, tired and gasping from exertion, while being covered in a thick, binding dust, mixing with your sweat to form a resilient glue.

Not every brewery was set up this way, some have—and Ninkasi also eventually bought—a *grain auger*. This machine is a medium between you and the mill. You pour malt into the auger bin, which then, at a desired pace, pumps the grain into the mill. Brilliant! No more gas mask and hours spent chiseling the grain crust off your skin at night.

At the homebrew level, you're milling at a much smaller capacity and require a tiny mill. The ones sold at homebrew shops are convenient and usually mount/clamp on the edge of a counter or workbench. Some home mills can be found economically at thrift, homestead, or craft shops and are operated by hand.

It can be physically demanding to hand crank your malt; the rotary motion lends to arm fatigue. I have an old-school Zassenhaus hand-crank coffee grinder. It can prove exhausting to simply churn out the few scoops of whole coffee beans for a sixteen-ounce French press! I don't use this for milling malt. But the marvels of the modern home brewer have presented the brewing community with a fun and innovative solution. The crank arm of the mill can be removed and replaced with the female end of an electrical hand drill bit, allowing the drill to perform the exerting rotations for you!

And if you want, you can still
wear the gas mask,
though it's probably not necessary.

Grist: True Grist

It would be too easy if you needed to grind that grain any old way and size. Unfortunately, malt requires a milling process precise enough to crush but not pulverize. The mashing process ends in lautering; but remember that the remaining part of the husk is necessary to perform a vital function. The mill then, requires a certain amount of dialing in.

There are two or more adjustable blades or burs inside the mill; the space between them is what you adjust to determine your ideal grist size, or size of the malt produced by the mill. Depending on what you're brewing, the grist size will reflect the result.

Mashin/Mashout/ Sparging/Lautering

We've talked about the concept of mashing. Now let's put it into play. Begin with the pile of milled/malted barley we've got (in the neighborhood of eight to fifteen pounds). After your DIY mash tun is assembled and sanitized, get that strike water ready. Once you've achieved your ideal temp of *152–160°F*, it's time to mash in!

How much water to use for your strike is something brewers spend years dialing in. The thought is, generally, folks are brewing approximately a five-gallon batch. Water ratio is important as is having a reasonable grasp of how heat and evaporation affect the brewing process. This will take some trial and error and approximation in the meantime. Use your noggin, and keep it simple.

Hot water evaporates much more quickly than cold water, so right off the bat, your strike water is losing volume. Most home brewers agree that the ideal ratio is *1.2–1.5 quarts* of water to each pound of grain. Over the many generations of brewers the world has seen, I bet this is a fair stab at accuracy. The general consensus seems to be, and what has worked for me, is to use half of your total water volume in your strike. Although some have made beer a science of perfection, it's always improving and takes many forms, all of them a little different, so play around. If you want to use a little more or a little less water, go for it! It's only beer!

A Helpful Tip I Learned The Hard Way

When adding the malt into the strike water (you know it's time because you used your thermometer), do not pour it all in at once. Pour slowly and consistently and giving it a stir with your elongated and handy (sanitized) spoon.

> *But what about the other half of the water...? Patience.*

A popular question is, "How long should my mash last?" This too will eat up a lot of time in the trial and error department. The **first forty-five minutes** of the mash are typically the most important. It is during this period that those diastatic starches are converted into sugars. Many believe that there is a conversion plateau that happens around this time, fewer starches convert to sugars after a point, so don't worry about it terribly. You can mash the wort for forty-five minutes or three hours, if you like. Read forums, ask questions, and do some trial and error on that mash!

★ ★ ★ ★ ★ ★ ★ ★ ★ ★

There is a lot of stainless steel in a brewery, and beer can be a messy business. In order to keep up with a demanding production schedule, brewery workers, commonly known as "cellar-folk," must maintain a cleaning schedule around the brews in order to keep the tanks in rotation. As soon as a tank becomes available, a fermenter or a bright tank (used to condition the beer after leaving the fermenter), we would have to clean those monsters and do it quick! Some of these tanks, especially the fermenters, can be extremely difficult to clean. Fortunately there is a caustic cleaner available, which is diluted with hot water to decimate any particulate particles in the tank. There is, however, a great and ominous fear of this chemical in the heart of any brewery worker. This stuff can make folk a little on edge.

One afternoon, one of our brewers was on a ladder, climbing up to the top of one of our tanks, probably performing a CIP: clean-in-place. Example: "Erik, did you CIP Fermenter 5?" "Yep, she's clean and ready to go!" Well, they must have knocked a hose loose with the ladder, because there was a terrific burst and the brewer suddenly was saturated by a seemingly endless flow of fluid. Assuming his fate, he proceeded to flail and scream, while we grabbed hoses and began blasting the poor devil. This particular caustic agent can be neutralized by a diluted peracetic acid, so water may not have been the most ideal choice. Nonetheless, after the initial shock, we were delighted to realize that our beloved was not melting from this horrible caustic agent, but instead, had merely busted our glycol line, containing a sugary liquid used by our in-line refrigeration system which kept our tanks cold and is quite harmless! But the scene had, by now, attracted onlookers, and to all of our humiliation, we learned about not living in a constant fear, less you risk manifesting it!

Remember that the temperature is relatively important. You want to keep that mash temp as close to **150–155°F** as possible throughout the duration of the mash. This is where the probe thermometer comes in handy; it allows you to keep a lid on your mash tun while maintaining a firm eye on the temperature.

Lautering

Until this point, the wort has been steeping away, in a cozy container, alone and untouched. *Lautering* clarifies the wort, by filtering the liquid wort from the oatmeal-like mash. Some brewers find lautering unnecessary and have different methods, but I believe it was a fantastic advent in the brewing of beer. Lautering is a hands-on, tiered, and staged process. It's sometimes two stages but some brewers use a third stage, the mashout. First, let's focus on the other two.

Tannins and the Vorlauf

Tannins are little buggers which lautering helps control. Another German word, they are a bitter/astringent compound, which thrive on proteins and agents created and released in the brewing process. Lautering, something of a fancy rinse, helps to avoid hyperactivity of these tannins, which can make your brew taste bitter and nasty.

To begin, put the liquid wort into your kettle, add cold water, and heat to a boil. Remember the stainless steel hose we installed on the mash tun? This is when its power gleams through the muck!

The first stage in lautering is recirculation. Once your mash is complete, let it sit for a few minutes before you begin. Does anyone have a beaker or a fancy Pyrex measuring cup? You are going to need a vessel, ideally one quart, preferably with a handle and a pouring spout, to burp the beer! Using that ball valve, fill the vessel with your wort carefully. The stainless steel hose acts as a filter, allowing the wort to pass, undisturbed by the floating mashy particles, appearing relatively unclouded in your vessel. Pour the vessel full of wort back on top of the mash bed. This process is called *vorlauf* (PRONOUNCED VOR-LOF).

This stage is essential. The recirculation process, or vorlauf, helps clarify the wort. Once we begin our sparge, the transfer from the mash tun to the kettle will be a lot easier, cleaner, and the wort will be tempered to provide maximum potential for deliciousness. Continue to draw approximately one quart of wort and pour it back onto the grain bed, slowly and carefully, a few times. The objective is to disturb the grain bed as little as possible. Perform between one and three times, until you're looking at something close to clear liquid. There will be particulates in the liquid, but each pull should be less cloudy than the previous.

The Sparge

The *sparge* is the big rinse that enormously reduces the risk of *stuck mash*. Similar to vorlauf, you're going to pour liquid on top of the grain bed, but with hot water, sprinkled as evenly as possible. Remember, in extract brewing, when we used a seven-gallon kettle to boil our wort? You're going to move the wort into it. The best way to accomplish this is to tier your brewery so your kettle is situated below your mash tun, so you can move the liquid with gravity.

The sparge is rinsing the grain of all the essential sugars, and in such a way as to provide the full value of body to your brew. As the sparge progresses, the wort drains into the kettle, and the

- CUT SMALL HOLES IN A MILK JUG. FILL IT WITH WATER AND HOLD IT OVER THE GRAIN BED. RINSE AND REPEAT UNTIL YOU HAVE THE DESIRED VOLUME IN YOUR KETTLE.

— or —

- ATTACH A HOSE WITH SMALL HOLES IN IT TO SOME PVC PIPE. USING SOME PVC TUBES AND ELBOWS, CREATE A LOOP WITH AN OPENING FOR A HOSE. SUSPEND THIS OVER THE GRAIN BED TO GIVE IT A SHOWER!

— or —

- FIND SOMETHING FOOD GRADE AND LIGHT, LIKE A COOKIE SHEET OR LARGE METAL TRAY WITH SMALL HOLES DRILLED IN IT. THIS WILL BE USED TO CREATE A BARRIER BETWEEN YOUR GRAIN BED AND THE SPARGE WATER YOU'RE ADDING TO IT. THE BARRIER SHOULD NOT TOUCH THE MASH. FIND A WAY TO SUSPEND THE BARRIER ABOVE THE GRAIN BED, OR USE A BARRIER LARGE ENOUGH TO SIT ON TOP OF THE MASH TUN.

mash condenses into a thick cake. The water slowly exiting the mash is made possible by the consistency of the grist.

The remaining half of your water not used in the mash will be used for sparging. If you were to simply open the valve on the bottom of our mash tun, chances are you would get the dreaded stuck mash. The powerful suction, caused by the top pressure of the mash, would clog the tiny valve.

So instead, while this is being performed, open the valve, only slightly. You want the tiniest trickle of wort; draining into the kettle. Continue until you have five to five and a half gallons of wort in your kettle. Your sparge, if done properly, should take forty-five minutes to an hour.

The barrier should have holes spread evenly enough so that when water passes through it, it's trickling over the top of the entire grain bed. This will more or less guarantee that the grain bed is sparged consistently, extracting the maximum amount of goodness. Using the suspended milk jug with holes in it (see sidebar) is rad too, as long as it's poured slowly across the grain bed! Just make sure that the water is good and warm. Warm water keeps the sparge moving. If it weren't for warm water, the sparge would stick!

Here is A Good Trick: If you've got a warm/not ice-cold can or bottle of something you intend to drink for refreshment, get a container of ice water and submerge the beverage. Spin the vessel rapidly for about a minute, voila! Instant, well, near instant drinkability!

The brewery environment is loaded with terrible tales of woe and despair about stuck mash. In larger commercial brew systems, when transfer of the wort from the mash tun to the kettle becomes stuck, there's little you can do but hope. If the worst case emerges for the wort, and nothing can be done, the brewer must make a difficult call: to dump or not to dump. The brewer must abandon brew sometimes if there is little hope of moving the volumes of wort into the kettle without destroying the precious life balance of the would-be beer. I've seen it happen; thirty barrels of brew is washed down the drain. My every intention is to spare you from the pain and agony of this—it might be best to stand back and attempt to commiserate from a safe distance. Careful diligence and a proper (not too small) grist size, will add to your favor in avoidance of such a fate. Once your kettle has reached approximately five to five and a half gallons, you're ready to begin your boil!

How many gallons is 30 barrels?

Boil

Now that your wort has safely made the trip from the mash tun to the kettle, it's time to crank up the heat! Most of the hard work is done and your mash is safe. You now add your hops! Once your brew reaches a boil, toss in the first round. **Remember:** Every batch of beer will differ in as many ways as you can change any step of the process: the time of boil, the length of the sparge, the amount of time required to reach a boil, etc. Additionally from brew to brew, the ingredients will differ, so keep a **log**. *(See the back of the book for one.)*

Most brews require the first hop addition at the initial sign of a boil. If there are any additions, they will vary considerably in amount, and the time between them. The boil, depending on the brew, can last one hour if it's ale or lager, or up to three hours if it's a barleywine, with differing hop additions for each. So this is a terrific opportunity to experiment. Go crazy! Once you've made a batch or two, have as many or as few hop additions as you wish and at intervals you deem fit.

✴ ✴ ✴ ✴ ✴   ✴ ✴ ✴ ✴ ✴

Scorching And Boil-Over

Wort has a tendency to stick to the bottom of the kettle and char-up if you're not giving it enough attention. The boil will require just enough maintenance, love, and care that you should never be too far away. A good rule of thumb is to keep a spoon handy and give the boil an occasional stir, taking extra care to ensure that the bottom gets ran over with the spoon every now and then. Another terrific idea is to keep a spray bottle of clean tap water. The boil is going to roar and gurgle and churn, and as the time marches on, the potential for a frothy, foamy top layer can form and build intensity. The spray bottle is to spray the foamy "head-like" substance attempting to take over your brewery. Spray it and it dissipates.

Boil to Fermenter

After an arduous adventure, you're ready to cut that heat! After all of your hop additions and careful consideration to your boil, you're ready for either fancy wort chiller or an ice bath. If you're using wort chiller, turn off the heat, follow the instructions from the team at your local homebrew shop, and plop that copper beauty in your brew.

If you're using an ice bath, carefully lift your kettle, place it into the bath, and commence stirring. Use your thermometer to monitor the brew until it's down to your yeast pitching temperature. Once you've arrived in your happy zone, get the yeast ready. It's also time to get whatever you're using for a fermenter ready. Sanitize that baby during your boil. Using a steady hand, hold your funnel over your fermenter, and grab a friend to help move the brew from the kettle to the fermenter. This can be a messy business, and difficult, as the kettle will be quite heavy. Have some towels in place on the floor and extra support if the kettle gets too heavy.

Once you've transferred the entire contents into your fermenter, it's time to pitch the yeast! If you've got one of those cool smack packs *(see chapter one, extract brewing)*, smack it now. Regardless, it's time to agitate it. Just like extract brew, get that vessel on your lap and rock it back and forth for a couple minutes, or until fatigued. This is the most important time you want to oxygenate your beer. Then attach your air lock and find a warm, dark place to store your brew. It's alive!

Answer from previous page: 1,650

Remember that the beer is going to burp and glug and become a strange sight and sound. Unless you love an uncouth and sporadic death rattle, keep it somewhere that you also don't spend a lot of time.

In just a matter of hours that beer will begin to off gas that CO_2 and it will go on for days. Ideally, your initial fermentation will last about a week. Keep a regular eye on it. Once the burping and the churning begins to settle out, it's about time to consider a secondary fermentation vessel: keg, bottles, another carboy, or a chosen depository. It's up to you, play around and experience the variations for each result.

⊢———DIY Yeast Starter

With the advent of modern yeast vials, powders, and smack packs, the homebrew is ultimately more inclined towards successful and efficient fermentation than ever before. Although these methods get the job done, there are other methods to consider that might help you understand the process more. It's understood in the professional brewing world, that control and perfection of your yeast is vital to the continuity and health of your brew. Having your own starter maximizes the control you hold over your brew. The yeast is so sacred to many breweries that they keep the stuff under lock and key. Some Trappist breweries give only the most select access to the yeast strain, which is sometimes as old as the brewery itself, and only the brewmaster may know its properties.

As long as conditions are optimal and you keep feeding it, you could keep yeast alive indefinitely. Making your own yeast makes sense if you intend to brew more frequently. Like all things in brewing, it's all about ratios.

Water : Malt Yeast : Volume

As every batch of beer you'll brew will have its differences, however subtle, they will be present in each result. Thus the amount of yeast you pitch will vary considerably from batch to batch. It may not always be ideal to toss in a full vial, or a whole smack pack.

When it boils down to it, we're looking for yeast cell counts in the billion! Just how many billion cells are required for a five-gallon batch will vary considerably between the different beer varietals. Having a yeast lab would violate the space philosophy I have in my tiny Portland apartment but that's not to discourage those who have a better understanding of micro or macro biology. If you've got the skills or are building them up, manipulating and maintaining your yeast strain at the base level is pretty rad! But for now, let's assume you're just looking to create an average but effective yeast starter to throw into your next homebrew.

*Have you ever created a bread starter? It's similar,
except here, we're going to bring it to a boil first.
Begin the process a full day before your brew!*

What You'll Need:

- **STERILE GLASS/PLASTIC STORAGE CONTAINER (ABOUT TWO LITER)**
- **MALT: DRY OR LIQUID (RATIO SHOULD BE EQUAL PARTS POUNDS TO WATER: ONE HALF POUND OF MALT TO ONE HALF GALLON OF WATER; INCREASE BY 20-25% IF YOU'RE USING THE LIQUID EXTRACT)**
- **WATER (ABOUT TWO LITERS)**
- **YEAST (ONE VIAL OR SMACK PACK)**
- **STOVE**
- **POT**
- **AN ICE BATH IN YOUR SINK**

Mix your water and malt until the malt is dissolved in the pot. Bring the liquid to a boil and cut the heat. Move the pot immediately into the ice bath. Once you reach about **70-90° F**, add your yeast and give it a good shake. Let this sit for a full 24 hours before you brew. Many homebrew activists out there use foil to cover the starter, which is a good idea. Cut the foil to size and fold it over the top!

Take a Gravity Reading

What is the specific gravity of your beer?

The specific gravity is the ratio of the water to other substances. In our case, we are measuring the specific gravity of the alcohol in the liquid. The best way to find this out is with a graduated cylinder and a hydrometer. The first reading is taken before you add your yeast to the wort. It measures the amount of fermentable sugars present for the yeast to munch on and convert into bliss. Fill the graduated cylinder with wort, insert the hydrometer, and give it a good spin. Once it stops spinning, look at the liquid level and make a note. This reading is known as the *original gravity (OG)*. Your next reading is taken after your fermentation is complete and is referred to as the *finishing gravity (FG)*. Take the reading in the same way. The difference between the two readings will be your percentage of alcohol. Your hydrometer should come with a conversion chart to help you in establishing your alcohol content.

It's important to note, that when you're recording your measurement to account for the liquid *meniscus* (the curve on the surface of the liquid caused by surface tension; *image on page 89*). The curve can be upward or downward, or concave or convex if you prefer. Be sure to record the measurement at the lowest point of liquid contact, as liquid will cling to the sides of the hydrometer.

Just in case, this website is quite useful: *brewersfriend.com/abv/calculator/*

Compare variations between batches and see how you can achieve the desired results.

There is a great vagueness with percentages and differences between readings. My primary consideration is the wide diversity of hopes and ideals between brewers. If it's something that interests you, read up on gravity readings to become comfortable measuring your own brew. You have tremendous potential to control these readings once you master the mechanics of them.

You can also take as many gravity readings as you like. You can even monitor the fermentation process with these and use the readings to determine when to stop fermenting or know you still have some time before it's ready. In the industry they are taken every day on the fermenters, watching and waiting for the beer to "dry out" or reach the desired gravity reading, determining that the beer is in fact finished!

Racking

If you recall, this funny word means to transfer the beer from the fermenter to the final conditioning vessel, like a keg or a bottle. This is the last stage the beer will endure before it hits your palate. Kegs are pretty darn cool. If you just have a keg and a CO2 tank to attach to it, that works. If you or anyone you know has a kegerator, then you're set, but most people don't. For this reason, most home brewers, myself included, like to bottle the goods. It makes them simple to give to your friends and generally easier to share. Which ever method you're into, once the fermentation has peaked, and you've moved your brew into your secondary, you've still got two weeks to two months before it's ready to drink! *For bottles, please refer to the extract section for carbonation, page 56.*

Congratulations! ├────────────────┤

You've brewed your beer, fermented your beer, and conditioned your beer; you're a homebrewer! There is still tons of experience to accrue and lessons to learn. I hope the resources in this book, if they haven't answered all your questions, will help to direct you how to get out there on your own and understand what you are looking for. There are endless resources out there; and many simple and direct questions can be quickly answered on Google.

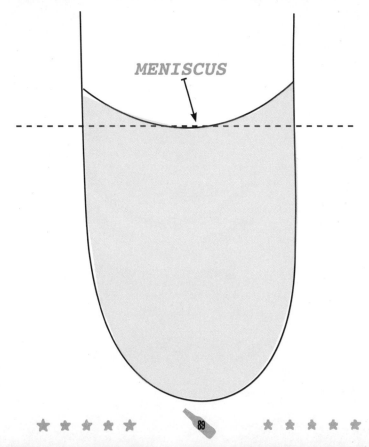

MENISCUS

Recipes by Jamie Floyd

Once you learn how to make a clean extract beer, you can choose to add the element of mashing the grains and using enzymes to create your own combinations of sugars and flavors. Now the base grains you use will help create distinct flavors based on the grain sourced and the conditions you set in the mash tun. These all-grain recipes are beers I have made on a professional scale and were downsized to home brew batch size for you to have some fun with.

- THE "PLATO SCALE" IS A DIFFERENT GRAVITY READING THAT HAS NO LINEAR RELATIONSHIP TO SPECIFIC GRAVITY. ONE DEGREE ON THE PLATO SCALE EQUALS ROUGHLY FOUR "BREWER'S POINTS." IT MEASURES PERCENTAGE OF EXTRACT BY WEIGHT. IT EXPRESSES DENSITY AS A PERCENTAGE OF SUCROSE BY WEIGHT. THE ADVANTAGE OF PLATO OVER SPECIFIC GRAVITY IS THAT IT TELLS YOU HOW MUCH FERMENTABLE MATERIAL YOU ARE WORKING WITH. IT IS MORE TYPICALLY USED IN EUROPEAN BREWING. SOMETIMES YOU'LL SEE PLATO READINGS IN BEER NAMES.
- "SRM" IS ANOTHER FANCY TERM THAT SIMPLY MEANS "STANDARD REFERENCE METHOD." IT IS A WAY TO TALK ABOUT THE COLOR OF THE BEER.

Starchile Pale:

Starchile was the first recipe I was allowed to design as a professional brewer at Steelhead Brewing Company. Sean Donnely and Teri Farhendorf allowed me to make a beer and I chose to do an experimental brew with a new grain being imported into the U.S. for the first time in 1995. Biscuit Malt had been used in Europe for a long time but was new to us and I made this recipe to see what the malt was like. This is one way to research new ingredients. If you use a familiar malt then it is easy to see what the new malt contributes to the beer. I liked the toasty and bready flavor from the Biscuit malt as well as its ability to dry out the finish in a beer. I have used this malt to create these flavors in other beers as well. I brewed the popular Starchile for the duration of my tenure at Steelhead which shows that experiments can work out the first time! It is also my first music tribute beer as Starchile is George Clinton's Superhero ego for Parliament, the protector of the Pleasure Principle. Bring some funk to your brewday. One Nation under a brew!

1.054 OG
32 IBUS
SRM: 9

Batch size: 5 gallons

Total Grain: 13.65 lbs.

Anticipated OG: 1.063

Plato: 15.36

Pre-boil amounts:
Evaporation Rate:
7.93 gallons per hour

Pre-Boil Wort Size: 13 gallons

Pre-boil Gravity: OG 1.024, Plato 6.2

Malt:

12 lbs. Great Western Pale

1.5 lbs. Castle Biscuit (or other)

.15 lbs. Baird Crystal 50/60

Hops:

.25 oz. Centennial 10.5 Alpha giving 9.2 IBUS, 60 minute addition

.25 oz. Nugget 13.0 Alpha giving 11.4 IBUS, 60 minute addition

.50 oz. Centennial 10.5 Alpha giving 11.2 IBUS, 20 minute addition

.25 oz. Liberty 4.5 Alpha giving 0 IBUS, Kettle off

Yeast:

Fullers or Chico

Bytor's Bane:

This is another early music tribute. I brewed this beer to take with my friends Mike and Barry when we took an RV to go see two back to back nights of Rush. Bytor and the Snow Dog is an epic battle between good and evil near the Nordic entrance to hell in which our hero Bytor prevails. This beer is also helpful for experimenting with hops. This time the beer has one hop variety in several additions. Glacier hops were a newer hop and seemed appropriate for the setting of the epic battle. It is also one of the first beers that I used flaked barley to make for a creamier mouthfeel. You can use the same base recipe and switch hops to see how each hops impacts a beer.

Malt:

11 lbs. Great Western Pale

1.75 lbs. Great Western Munich

.75 lbs. Briess Caramel 40L

.33 lbs. Flaked Barley

Hops:

2.0 oz. Glacier 6.0 Alpha giving 44.6 IBUS, 60 minute addition

2.0 oz. Glacier 6.0 Alpha giving 25.3 IBUS, 20 minute

2.0 oz. Glacier 6.0 Alpha giving 0 IBUS, Kettle off

2.0 oz. Glacier 6.0 Alpha giving 0 IBUS, Dry Hop

Yeast:

London Ale or Chico

1.064 OG
70 IBUS
SRM: 9

Batch size: 5 gallons

Total Grain: 13.83 lbs.

Anticipated OG: 1.063

Plato: 15.7

Boil time: 60 minutes

Pre-boil Amounts: Evaporation Rate: 7.9 gallons per hour

Pre-Boil Wort Size: 16.89 gallons

Pre-boil Gravity: OG 1.019, Plato 4.83

Clover Leaf Irish Ale:

Irish Red Ales have deeper caramel and toffee flavors than an ESB as well as a touch of roasted flavor without being stout-like. Malty like a Scottish Ale but not as hoppy as a British or U.S. Ale, this beer is appealing to malt heads. You can swap out different pale-base malts or caramel to see how each maltster creates different grains. This is also an excellent alternative to an Irish Stout or the dreaded green beers of St. Patrick's Day.

1.063 OG
38 IBUS
SRM:12.5

Batch size: 5 gallons

Total Grain: 13.75 lbs.

Anticipated OG: 1.063

Plato: 15.4

Boil Time: 60 minutes

Pre-boil amounts:
Evaporation Rate:
7.93 gallons per hour

Pre-Boil Wort Size:
12.93 gallons

Pre-boil Gravity: OG
1.024, Plato 6.15

Malt:

11 lbs. Briess Pale Malt

2 lbs. Briess Victory

.50 lbs. Briess Caramel 80L

.25 lbs. Briess Special Roast

Hops:

.75 oz. Centennial 9.0 Alpha
giving 23.7 IBUS, 60 minutes

.75 oz. Centennial 9.0 Alpha
giving 14.3 IBUS, 20 minutes

1.0 oz. Mt. Hood 6.5 Alpha
giving 0 IBUS, Kettle off

1.0 oz. Mt. Hood 6.5 Alpha
giving 0 IBUS, Dry Hop

Yeast:

London or Scottish Ale

Piccadilly ESB:

It's a good idea to try one style of beer in both extract and all-grain forms. They are not meant to be the same but rather to show that one style can have different flavors. Each brewer is an artist and a scientist so how we each make our own recipes guides the eventual flavors. I have made eight to ten different ESBs over the years. They all have some basic similarities as styles do but they are all unique unto themselves. This one features Maris Otter from Crisp and have Challenger instead of Fuggles as in the extract brew. Make them both and taste the differences.

Malt:

11.5 lbs. Crisp Maris Otter Pale malt

1.5 lbs. Munich

.75 lbs. Briess Special Roast

.75 lbs. Briess Caramel 40 L

Hops:

.75 oz. Challenger 8.2 Alpha giving 21.1 IBUS, 60 minute addition

1.0 oz. Challenger 8.2 Alpha giving 17.1 IBUS, 20 minutes

1.5 oz. East Kent Goldings 4.75 Alpha giving 0 IBUS, Kettle Off

1.0 oz. East Kent Goldings 4.75 Alpha giving 0 IBUS, Dry Hop

Yeast:

London Ale of other English Style yeast strain

1.064 OG
38 IBUS
SRM:12

Batch size: 5 gallons

Total Grain: 14.5 lbs.

Anticipated OG: 1.066 Plato: 16.7

Boil time: 60 minutes

Pre-boil Amounts:
Evaporation Rate:
7.93 gallons per hour

Pre-Boil Wort Size:
12.9 gallons

Pre-boil Gravity: OG
1.025, Plato 6.43

Hops for Hay:

Owner of the Bier Stein and former Eugene Brewer, Chip Hardy and I made Hops for Hay while working at Steelhead together. We made it in honor of Glen Hay Falconer, legendary Eugene brewer and one of our best friends. This beer was made for the Sasquatch Brewers Festival that we helped start to remember Glen and raise money for Brewing Scholarships and local charities. We made a beer that Glen would like so we emulated his style of brewing using grains and hop varieties. Sometimes you just make a beer and not a style. By experimenting with different ingredients you begin to develop the ability to make flavors you desire more than to recreate other styles from the past. It is ok to come up with your own recipe and express yourself the way Glen always did. And as he would always say: When in doubt, add more hops! Raise a home brewed beer with your friends whenever you can. Those memories will last a lifetime!

1.063 OG
54 IBUS
SRM: 9

Batch size: 5 gallons

Total Grain: 11 lbs.

Anticipated OG: 1.066

Plato: 16.12

Boil Time: 60 minutes

Pre-boil amounts:
Evaporation Rate:
7.93 gallons per hour

Pre-Boil Wort Size:
12.9 gallons

Pre-boil Gravity: OG
1.026, Plato 6.45

Malt:

4.5 lbs. Crisp Maris Otter Pale

4.5 lbs. Great Western Pale

1.0 lbs. Great Western Munich

.5 lbs. Briess Caramel 80L

.5 lbs. Briess Carapils

Hops:

.50 oz. Chinook 13.0 Alpha giving 20.1 IBUS, Frist Wort addition

.75 oz. Willamette 5.0 Alpha giving 12.9 IBUS, 60 minute addition

1.0 oz. Amarillo 10.0 Alpha giving 20.8 IBUS, 20 minute addition

2.0 oz. Crystal 3.2 Alpha giving 0 IBUS, Kettle off

1.0 oz. Amarillo 10.0 Alpha giving 0 IBUS, Dry Hop

1.0 oz. Crystal 3.2 Alpha giving 0 IBUS, Dry Hop

Yeast:

London Ale or Chico

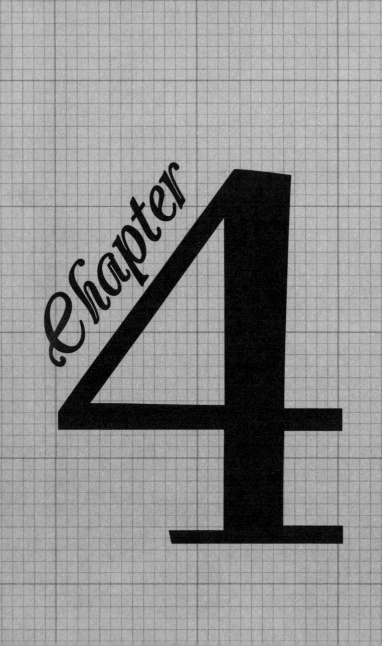

BEFORE
AND
AFTER
THOUGHTS

Kegs

There are different types of kegs. The most common in the homebrew world are five and one half gallon tubes called *Cornelius Kegs*, or *Corny kegs*. These typically have a line-in for your CO2, a line out for your beer and a large oval opening for pouring in the brew. You can find Corny kegs in larger and smaller sizes. These look like soda kegs found in restaurants.

There are also what's known as *Pony Kegs*. These look like a fifteen and a half gallon commercial keg, but only hold seven and a half gallons. These do not have in and out lines like Corny kegs. Instead they have a single line that attaches to a coupler (which has a line in and line out) inside a kegerator or a major CO2 line like you'll see at bars or restaurants. Visit your local homebrew shop to take a look at your options.

What is a Kegerator?

Feeling industrious? There are as many ways to build your own kegerator as there are stars in the sky. A *kegerator* is a converted refrigerator, designed to hold a keg. Start by going to thrift stores and finding a fridge that both works and is large enough to fit your keg. Sometimes people build their kegerator to house the CO2 system as well as the beer. Some construct them with the CO2 outside of the fridge. There are countless forums, sites, instructions, and insights for building these things so I'm only including a brief guide to get you started.

First, pull out the racks and make room for the keg. Drill a hole for your tap. Run some gaskets and hose(s) to your CO2 source and keg. If you store your CO2 source on the outside, you'll need to drill another hole for the hose.

The cost can add up:

- **FRIDGE**
- **HOSE**
- **TAP**
- **COUPLER**
- **CO2**
- **CO2 TANK**
- **CO2 REGULATOR**
- **KEG**
- **GASKETS AND FITTINGS**

Many of these parts can be obtained cheaply if you aren't in a hurry. And you can find used and homemade kegerators on Craigslist as well. Good luck!

Finishing Thoughts:

BREWING BEER IS A STAPLE OF HUMAN CIVILIZATION.

WE CAN ALL SHARE IN THE GRATITUDE THAT WE NO LONGER HAVE TO SIT AROUND A CAULDRON AND SPIT INTO THE BREW TO HELP THE BEER ALONG!

IDEAS PRESS ON INTO THE FUTURE AND CONSTANTLY CHANGE.

FOR BETTER OR WORSE WE HUMANS FIND SOMETHING WE LIKE DOING AND CONTINUE DOING IT UNTIL WE BELIEVE WE'VE REACHED SATISFACTION.

★ ★ ★ ★ ★ ★ ★ ★ ★ ★

NO MATTER HOW PERFECT SOMETHING IS, THERE'S ALWAYS ROOM FOR IMPROVEMENT.

I TRULY HOPE THAT YOU HAVE FOUND SOMETHING THAT MAKES SENSE TO YOU AND HAS PROVEN USEFUL.

TAKE COMFORT THAT THIS IS BUT ONE OF MANY RESOURCES TO HELP YOU REACH YOUR GOALS.

TAKE ALL THE TIME YOU NEED TO WORK OUT YOUR IDEAL METHOD.

HAVE A BLAST EVERY STEP OF THE WAY!

⭐ ⭐ ⭐ ⭐ ⭐ 103 ⭐ ⭐ ⭐ ⭐ ⭐

Glossary

ABV: Alcohol By Volume

Air lock: A device used to block airflow, typically equipped with an air bubble to maintain pressure.

All-Grain Brewing: The brewing of beer in which you create your mash from raw malt.

Autolysis: When the yeast runs out of delicious food to eat, turns on itself, and does the unforgivable, resulting in an off flavor. (or yeast cannibalism)

Capper: A device used to apply the cap to your bottle of brew!

Carboy: (*or Fermenter*) A large glass/plastic container for storing and fermenting beer.

Chill Haze: A cloudy effect which occurs when you are conditioning the beer at near freezing temperature giving the impression that the beer is not filtered properly but is ultimately not a bad thing.

Concentrated Malt Extract: A sweet-tasting concentration from mashing, the process of combining a mix of milled grain and water.

Cornelius Kegs or Corny kegs: The most common five and one half gallon storage kegs. These typically have a line-in for your CO_2, a line out for your beer and a large oval opening for pouring in the brew. You can find Corny kegs in larger and smaller sizes. These look like soda kegs found in restaurants.

Diastatic Enzymes: *(starches)* Enzymes created during the germinating process in the grain. They convert starches into lovely fermentable sugars.

Extract Brewing: The brewing of beer using a malted extracted as your main malt source.

Fermenter: see carboy

FG: *(final gravity)* The last gravity reading taken once the beer has finished fermenting.

Full Boil: When you bring nearly six and a half gallons of water to a boil.

Germinating: The sprouting stage of a seed or spore.

Graduated Cylinder: A lab cylinder used for measuring liquid volume. For brewing they are used to take gravity readings with the help of a hydrometer.

Grain Auger: The machine acting as a medium between you and the mill. You pour malt into the auger bin, which then, at a desired pace, pumps the grain into the mill.

Grain Sock: A cloth bag which performs the task of holding separately, any grain, hops, or added element from the brew.

Gravity: Refers to the specific gravity or relative density compared to water; *i.e.: the relationship between water and the fermenting sugars*

Grist size: The term used to describe the condition of the grain after having endured the milling process. Different brews will call for different grist sizes.

Hops: A flavoring and stability agent for the beer.

Hop Pellet: They look like a large bright-green fish-food pellet or rabbit food.

Hot Liquor: Known to the rest of us as "hot water," is what is used for the strike.

Hydrometer: An instrument, which is commonly used to measure the density of a liquid.

IBU: International bitterness units; a fancy acronym commonly used to tell you how hoppy and bitter your beer is.

Kegerator: A converted refrigerator, designed to hold a keg and tap system.

Krausen: A yeast and protean foamy head that forms at the top of your fermentation vessel once you've pitched your yeast into your brew!

Lautering: The act of clarifying the wort, by filtering the liquid wort from the oatmeal-like mash.

Liquor Back: A temperature-controlled reservoir, which holds enough "hot liquor," to serve as your strike.

Mash: The steeping process

Mash Tun: The initial vessel used for steeping your grains to create your wort.

Mashing-in: The malted barley is dumped into the vessel containing the strike water, ideally a temperature-controlled mash tun.

Meniscus: The curve on the surface of the liquid caused by surface tension.

Milled Grain: Grain that has gone through the milling process and has reached its proper grist size.

Milling: A simple procedure but requires a fair amount of accuracy. The idea is to shape the malt so that the ideal amount of enzymes can be released in the mash.

OG: *(original gravity)* The first gravity reading taken at the completion of the brew.

Pitching: Adding your yeast

Plato: The ratio of fermentable sugars to water in the beer. The common measurement in the brewing industry, as opposed to specific gravity. Your choice, Plato simply requires a conversion, luckily there are many online calculators!

Pliny the Elder: (AD 23 – August 25, AD 79), born Gaius Plinius Secundus. A member of the Roman Empire, he spent his time as a naval commander, philosopher, naturalist, and writer.

Pony Kegs: These look like a fifteen and a half gallon commercial keg, but only hold seven and a half gallons.

Priming Sugar: Sugar used for carbonating beer.

Racking Bucket: A five-plus gallon bucket with an opening/closing valve at the bottom for attaching a hose and siphon so that you can transport your brew into its final home.

Session Beer: Low alcohol beer made for regular, long time consumption.

Siphon: A device, typically a tube, used to pull liquid from one place to another.

Small Batch: Beer brewed at the micro level and below.

Sparge: The big rinse that enormously reduces the risk of stuck mash.

Spent grain: The term used to describe the grain once it has been used for the mash.

SRM: A fancy term that simply means "standard reference method." It is a way to talk about the color of the beer.

Steep: A similar process to mashing, used to extract colors and flavors from certain grains.

Strike Water: The initial water used to create your mash or steep, a similar process to mashing, used to extract colors and flavors from certain grains.

Tannins: Another German word, they are a bitter/astringent compound, which thrive on proteins and agents created and released in the brewing process.

To Mill: The pulverizing of grain into a desired grist size. Typically done in a mill, between crushing burs.

To Rack: *(verb)* To transport your beer, once the condition is finished, into its final home. It could be a keg, bottle, or can.

Trappist: A style of beer originating in Belgium, It's tenets state that it must be made by monks, the brewing must be secondary to their faith, they can't really be in it for the profit, and it has to be brewed within the walls of the Trappist monastery.

According to the powers that be, there are currently only ten of these breweries in the world, most of them in Belgium.

Vorlauf: The drawing of some of the wort from the mash, acting as a recirculation process, prior to the sparge, helps clarify the wort.

Wort: *(pronounced wert)* The resulting fluid of steeping grains in your strike water for anywhere from 30-90 minutes.

Wort Chiller: A coil of copper tube with an in line and an out line. Both ends have a hose attachment; the line in attaches to your water source and the line out will drain. Cool water passes through the chiller, lowering the temperature of your wort rapidly.

Yeast Cake: The thick layer of yeast which collects in your fermenting beer.

★ ★ ★ ★ ★ ★ ★ ★ ★ ★

HOMEBREW TALK
homebrewtalk.com

**A REALLY INTERACTIVE LEARNING SITE:
CRAFTBEER.COM**

**PROBREWER.COM FOR
PLATO-SG CALCULATOR**
*probrewer.com/tools/beer-specifications-
calculator*

**TECHNOLOGY BREWING AND
MALTING BY WOLFGANG KUNZE**
(SPENDY AND INTENSELY INVOLVED!)
siebelinstitute.com

WYEAST LABORATORIES
wyeastlab.com

**HYDROMETER AND ALCOHOL
CONTENT (ABV) CALCULATOR**
brewersfriend.com/abvcalculator

**A REALLY INTERACTIVE LEARNING SITE:
CRAFTBEER.COM**

TERRIFIC PORTLAND-BASED HOMEBREW SHOP
F.H. STEINBART CO.
234 SE 12TH AVE, PORTLAND, OR 97214

———————————————————

THE BIER STEIN
AWESOME PLACE TO DRINK, EAT, AND BE MERRY
1591 WILLAMETTE ST. EUGENE, OR 97401

———————————————————

NINKASI BREWING COMPANY:
NINKASIBREWING.COM

———————————————————

IF THERE WAS AN "ACADEMY" IN THE STATES,
IT WOULD BE HERE:
SIEBELINSTITUTE.COM

———————————————————

GEARED TOWARDS BREWERIES, BUT TERRIFIC FOR
LEARNING AND NETWORKING:
HOPUNION.COM

———————————————————

A MORE ROBUST PLACE TO LEARN ABOUT AND ORDER
LARGE QUANTITIES OF MALT:
BREWINGWITHBRIESS.COM/DEFAULT.HTM

CONVERSION CHART

WEIGHT

METRIC		U.S.
1 GRAM	⟶	0.035 OUNCE
500 GRAMS	⟶	1.100 POUNDS
1 KILOGRAM (1,000 GRAMS)	⟶	2.200 POUNDS
1 TON	⟶	1,1923 TONS
1 TON	⟶	2,204.6 POUNDS

LIQUID MEASURE

METRIC		U.S.
1 LITER	⟶	2.113 PINTS
1 LITER	⟶	1.056 QUARTS
3.785 LITERS	⟶	1 GALLON

TEMPERATURE

FAHRENHEIT TO CELCIUS: SUBTRACT 32, MULTIPLY BY FIVE, THEN DIVIDE BY NINE.

CELCIUS			FAHRENHEIT
100 ⟷	212	⟷	BOILING TEMP
21 ⟷	70	⟷	ROOM TEMP
0 ⟷	32	⟷	FREEZING TEMP

BEWARE THE KRAUSEN

Brew

Logs

BREW LOG FOR EXTRACT BREWING:

type of beer	
ABV	
ingredients used	
strike water	
temperature	
mash in time	
different times for hop additions	
gravity readings	
notes for smell and taste	
observations during brewing process	

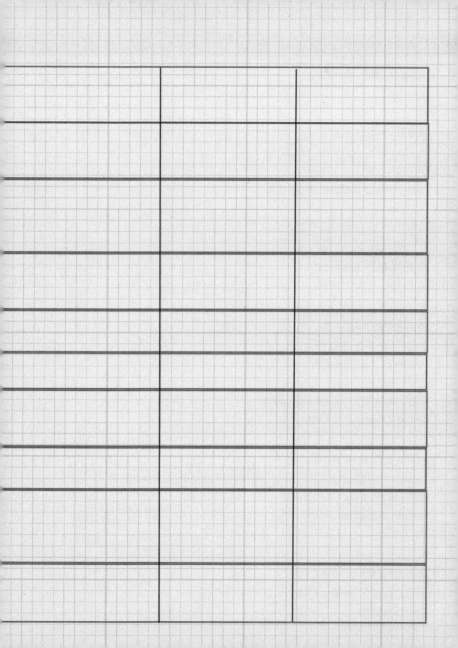

BREW LOG FOR EXTRACT BREWING:

type of beer	
ABV	
ingredients used	
strike water	
temperature	
mash in time	
different times for hop additions	
gravity readings	
notes for smell and taste	
observations during brewing process	

type of beer	
time and length of sparge	
ABV	
ingredients used	
strike water	
temperature	
mash in time	
different times for hop additions	
gravity readings	
notes for smell and taste	
observations during brewing process	

ᔐ ACKNOWLEDGEMENTS ᔐ

Credit for the successful completion of this book is due to a great many people (more than I can hope to list), as it is the result of many years of friendship, education, hard work, and guidance. I wish to extend my most sincere gratitude to Jamie Floyd for his generous contributions and the amazing recipes found herein. To Joe Biel of Microcosm Publishing for urging me to take pencil in hand. To my good friend, Josh Rein of Logboat Brewing in Columbia, Missouri, for showing me how easy it is to make a delicious beer at home! To my wife, Lauren, for showing me tremendous support along the many years of my tumultuous journey. I extend a warm hand to the hard-working team at Microcosm! I want to thank Ninkasi Brewing Company for giving me a chance to get involved. To the city of Prague for introducing me to the simplicity of delicious lagers and pilsners. Lastly to the Brewers of Pilsner Urquell for everything!

Erik Spellmeyer
is a former cellar-
man of Ninkasi
Brewing and has
been a long
time craft beer
enthusiast.

He is the head of sales and works
on title development at Microcosm
Publishing.

He lives in Portland, Oregon.

Jamie Floyd is part owner and founding brewer of Ninkasi Brewing Company and was the head brewer of Steelhead Brewing Company from 1997–2005.

He is a nationally known beer enthusiast living in Eugene, Oregon.